EVOLUTIONARY CHURCH:

RECLAIMING LOVE

AS RELIGION

EVOLUTIONARY CHURCH: RECLAIMING LOVE AS RELIGION

A HUMAN BEING IS A UNIQUE WORD IN THE COSMIC SCROLL

THE EVOLUTION OF OUR INTIMACY PARTICIPATES IN THE EVOLUTION OF THE INTIMATE UNIVERSE

• • •

From Conscious Evolution 1.0 to Conscious Eovlution 2.0

One Mountain, Many Paths: Oral Essays
Volume Fifteen

DR. MARC GAFNI AND
BARBARA MARX HUBBARD

Author: Marc Gafni and Barbara Marx Hubbard
Title: Evolutionary Church

Identifiers: ISBN 979-8-88834-064-6 (electronic)
ISBN 979-8–88834–063–9 (paperback)
Library of Congress Cataloging-in-Publication Data available

Edited by Timothy Paul Aryeh, Paul Bennett, Talya Bloom, and David Cicerchi

World Philosophy and Religion Press,
St. Johnsbury, VT

in conjunction with

IP Integral Publishers

https://worldphilosophyandreligion.org

JOIN THE REVOLUTION!

CONTENTS

EDITORIAL NOTE ABOUT AUTHORSHIP, EDITING, AND THE RADICAL CONTEXT FOR THIS SERIES

ORAL ESSAYS FROM THE ONE MOUNTAIN, MANY PATHS WEEKLY BROADCAST

This volume is part of the Oral Essays library, a series of lightly edited, compiled transcripts of oral teachings given by Dr. Marc Gafni and the late Barbara Marx Hubbard in their weekly online broadcast, One Mountain, Many Paths, which they co-founded in 2017. Originally called an "Evolutionary Church," One Mountain, Many Paths became a key venue for the articulation of an inspired and deeply grounded new Story of Value in response to the meta-crisis. Marc and Barbara—together with Zak Stein,1 Kristina Kincaid, Ken Wilber, Sally Kempton, Lori Galperin, Aubrey Marcus and dozens of other thought-leaders over the years—began to articulate what they call a World Philosophy and World Religion2 as a context for our diversity.

---

1 Zak, together with Ken Wilber, has been Marc's primary intellectual partner and an initiate lineage holder in CosmoErotic Humanism.

2 This project is grounded in four core organizational frameworks: 1) The Center for World Philosophy and Religion, co-founded by Marc Gafni, Zachary Stein, Sally Kempton, and Ken Wilber, and chaired over the years by John P. Mackey, Barbara Marx Hubbard, Aubrey Marcus, Gabrielle Anwar and Shareef Malnik, Carrie Kish and Adam Bellow, and Kathleen J. Brownback. 2) The Office for the Future, chaired by Stephanie Valcke and Ivan Bossyut. 3) The World Philosophy and Religion Press, founded and chaired by Aubrey Marcus, together with Marc Gafni and Zachary Stein. 4) The Foundation for Conscious Evolution, founded by Barbara Marx Hubbard and currently chaired by Peter Fiekowsky. For a complete list of key leadership, see the Office for the Future website, www.officeforthefuture.com.

Until Barbara's passing in 2019, she and Marc transmitted teachings together as evolutionary partners and "whole mates," weaving together insights and transmissions from their decades of practice, study, teaching, and activism into a synergy of wisdom, a grounded vision for future policy across all sectors of society.

Much of the *dharma* material below comes directly from Marc, so it was originally all in quotation marks—but that looked a little odd. So per his suggestion we removed them, and the reader should consider the paragraphs on the next several pages as one extended quote from him. We are joyfully grateful to Marc for the clarity of his *dharma*, the elegance and "second simplicity" of this language, and the mad, Outrageous Love with which he transmits his teachings.

Barbara and Marc called the mission of One Mountain "a Planetary Awakening in Evolutionary Love Through Unique Self Symphonies." We are an evolutionary community with a deeply grounded, radically alive, and "post-tragic" revolutionary spirit. We are activating a new humanity and awakening as a new species: Homo amor, the fulfillment of Homo sapiens.

One Mountain is committed to articulating a Story of Value that can become the ground for the new society that must be birthed in response to the meta-crisis. We recognize that we are living at a pivotal moment in history. In this "time between stories," the great moral imperative is to tell the new Story of Value. It is ours to do, personally and collectively, with great trembling and ecstatic joy.

FROM DOGMA TO *DHARMA*: ETERNAL AND EVOLVING FIRST PRINCIPLES AND FIRST VALUES

The teachings are grounded in decades of deep study across many wisdom traditions. Over the years, week by week, these teachings were incrementally developed within the framework of the One Mountain, Many Paths broadcast. We often refer to these teachings as *dharma*.

This word was originally used in lineage traditions to refer to something like universal law. This is a crucial realization: just as there is universal law in mathematical value, there is also a sense of universal law in ethics and value.

Historically, *dharma* often devolved into unchanging dogma. Evolution was ignored, and the natural process of *dharma* evolution became disconnected from its deep, eternal context. The weakness of the word *dharma* is that too often it did not include the evolving insights of the sciences, it confused local cultural truths with universal truths, and it used words like "eternal," as in "eternal Tao," as opposed to words like "evolution."

Eternal came to mean unchanging, and that kind of thinking often led to overly ethnocentric readings of *dharma*. Local systems would claim their religious and cultural insights as immutable, which stood in the way of the emergence of a genuine world Story of Value that is real, inherent to Cosmos, and backed by the Universe—even as it is also always evolving.

Or, as we often say, "eternal value is evolving value. The eternal Tao is the evolving Tao."

We have shown that, emergent from profound insights in the "interior sciences," eternal does not mean unchanging in time; it means what we call the deeper Field of ErosValue that is beneath culture, geography, and history, which lives beneath all individual and collective values, and beneath time and space itself.

As such, we have gradually transitioned from the term *dharma* to the term Value, in the sense of the Field of Value that lives beneath all values. This Field of Value discloses as First Principles and First Values embedded in a Story of Value.

Indeed, as the interior sciences knew and the exterior sciences imply, Reality arises in a Field of ErosValue in which an entire set of mathematical, musical, molecular, moral, and mystical values are the very ground of all being. That Field of Value is eternal—the true ground of the Good, True and Beautiful—even as it is evolving.

But of course, it is equally critical not just to talk about evolving value, but to ground the evolving value in its true nature, the eternal Field of First Principles and First Values, always reaching for ever-more life, ever-more love, ever-more care, ever-more depth, ever-more uniqueness, ever-more intimate communion, and ever-more transformation.

As such, when we refer to the word *dharma*, which still appears in these texts together with the word value, we refer to an evolving *dharma* grounded in an eternal and evolving Field of Value. Indeed, eternity and evolution are two faces of the whole, opposites joined at the hip, that characterize the nature of our Cosmos in virtually all of its expressions.

It's in these terms that we ground a robust world philosophy that integrates the validated, leading-edge insights of premodern traditional wisdom, modern wisdom, and more recent postmodern insights, weaving them together into a new whole greater than the sum of its parts.

This new whole is a shared Story of Value rooted in First Principles and First Values that are both eternal and evolving.

These First Principles and First Values of Cosmos are woven together into a new Story of Value as a context for our diversity, a new Universe Story. This new story gives us the best possible responses we have to the mystery, and to the great questions:

- Who am I? Who are we?
- Where am I? Where are we?
- What should I do? What should we do?

It is only through such a shared Universe Story—a narrative of identity and ethos as a context for our blessed diversity—that we can realize how what unites is so much greater than what divides us.

Only a new Story of Value will allow us to both respond to the meta-crisis and participate together in birthing the most true, good, and beautiful world that we already know is possible.

THIS ORAL ESSAYS SERIES IS AN ENTRYWAY TO THE GREAT LIBRARY OF COSMOEROTIC HUMANISM

This Oral Essays series is part of the overarching project of the Great Library at the Center for World Philosophy and Religion, led by Dr. Marc Gafni, together with Dr. Zak Stein. The aim of the Great Library project is to articulate a robust and comprehensive new Story of Value, CosmoErotic Humanism, in the form of dozens of well-researched and extensively footnoted academic works.

Our vision is to provide the philosophical framework that will be vital for navigating humanity through this time of immense crisis and transformation.

To begin your journey into CosmoErotic Humanism, we tenderly refer you to the book First Principles and First Values, co-authored by Marc Gafni, Zak Stein, and Ken Wilber, under the name David J. Temple. David J. Temple is a pseudonym created for enabling ongoing collaborative authorship at the Center for World Philosophy and Religion. The two primary authors behind David J. Temple are Marc Gafni and Zak Stein, and for different projects, specific writers will be named as part of the collaboration, such as Ken Wilber and others.

Three other volumes complete this introduction: A Return to Eros, by Marc Gafni and Kristina Kincaid; Your Unique Self, by Marc Gafni; and Education in a Time between Worlds, by Zak Stein.

We hope that the Oral Essays in the present volume, with their informal style of transmission, will serve as an allurement and entryway for you into the more formal books of the Great Library that provide the robust intellectual underpinnings of the new Story of Value.

A NOTE ABOUT THE EDITORS

This Oral Essays collection has been edited by students of the new Story of CosmoErotic Humanism. Each of us has actively participated in One Mountain, Many Paths, and most of us have been in deep "Holy of Holies" study with Dr. Marc Gafni for many years.

We have been privileged to find ourselves well-versed in the teachings, and even emerging as lineage-holders of CosmoErotic Humanism.3

We view this editing project as a privilege and a deep practice of study and clarification. We experience ourselves as a mystical editing society, frequently meeting and conversing together about the content—the depth of knowledge and wisdom offered here—as well as the technical intricacies involved with publishing a beautiful and coherent series of books. In so doing, we function as a "Unique Self Symphony," which itself is a Dharmic

---

3   CosmoErotic Humanism is a world philosophical movement aimed at reconstructing the collapse of value at the core of global culture. Much like Romanticism or Existentialism, CosmoErotic Humanism is not merely a theory but a movement that changes the very mood of Reality. It is an invitation to participate in evolving the source code of consciousness and culture towards a cosmocentric *ethos* for a planetary civilization.

The term CosmoErotic Humanism, initially coined by Dr. Gafni and colleagues, points to a complex, multi-faceted, layered, and nuanced evolutionary set of insights that has evolved over decades of intensive research, teaching, and spiritual practice from deep within a wide range of wisdom traditions (including the Wisdom of Solomon lineage tradition, Bodhisattva Buddhism, and Kashmir Shaivism), as well as multiple disciplines including complexity theory, chaos theory, emergence theory, molecular biology, and the more classical disciplines of the humanities.

The seeds of CosmoErotic Humanism were planted with Dr. Marc Gafni's work on a two-volume, 1,000-page opus called *Radical Kabbalah* (Integral Publishers, 2012). This scholarly work, sourced from deep study within the esoteric lineage texts of the Wisdom of Solomon, points to a non-dual, or acosmic, realization which—unlike the prevailing conceptualization of non-duality—does not efface the human being; rather, it is highly humanistic in its nature. The next step in the evolution of CosmoErotic Humanism was the insight that all of Reality is evolving Eros, which lives in, as, and through the human being.

A failure of Eros leads inexorably to the creation of narratives of "pseudo-eros." CosmoErotic Humanism is a response to the modern mental and social breakdown sourced in the proliferation of multiple forms of pseudo-eros and its broken narratives, such as rivalrous conflict governed by win/lose metrics and the dogmatic denial of intrinsic value in Cosmos, which together generate our current "global intimacy disorder."

term that connotes an omni-considerate collaboration between realized Unique Selves synergizing our unique gifts into a new emergence greater than the sum of the parts. Even as we worked diligently to standardize our editing styles, meeting on a weekly basis to debate the nuances of phrasing, we also operated from within a deep appreciation of the unique style that each editor brought to his or her work. As such, the reader might notice some variation in editing style among the books.

Please note that Dr. Marc Gafni has not reviewed these edited Oral Essays, as he is deeply engaged in writing the formal books of the Great Library. But he has been generous in responding to questions and providing overall guidance in the project. Overall, as Marc's students and students of the *dharma*, we have made it a key project at the Center to publish these pieces of work relatively independently.

OUR UNIQUE ORAL-ESSAY EDITING STYLE PRESERVES THE ENERGY OF THE ORIGINAL TRANSMISSION

Dr. Marc Gafni is a uniquely gifted teacher whose oral transmission is imbued with a quality that has proven transformative for his students. Many of us feel mystically transformed by both the content and the underlying energy of the transmission style. Therefore, as we like to say, trust the magic ways the *dharma* comes through your unique understanding!

As Marc's empowered students, colleagues, and beloved friends, we have a deep knowing that these teachings are vital for the survival and thriving of humanity as we know it, and we recognize the importance of publishing his teachings in a written format that will be accessible by future generations. At the same time, we sought to preserve the Eros of the original oral transmission with all of its nuance, power, and depth. Our intention in the editing process, to the greatest extent possible, has been to keep these spoken artifacts intact in order to maintain the flow of the original transmission. We have therefore chosen not to engage in intensive formal editing, as we found that doing so resulted in the loss of the energetic transmission that is so key to fully receiving the *dharma*.

After experimenting with many ways to present these texts, we developed a specific way of laying out the text on the page. Marc, in collaboration with Zak Stein and Russian intellectual/artist Elena Maslova-Levin—and ultimately all of the editors, through many conversations—developed a unique, artistic presentation of the text, using bolding, italics, bullet points, and other stylistic features which together serve to accentuate the immediacy of the oral transmission.

As part of this editing style, intended to preserve the integrity of the original transmission, we have refrained from removing the frequent recapitulations of key themes. We found that each recapitulation contributes something vital to the rhythm and music beneath the words, like the beating drum of our hearts. These recapitulations not only review previous material but also add important new emphases, perspectives, and elements of the new Story of Value. We ask for your patience as a reader to trust the rhythm of these texts, and we trust you as a reader to have the depth and steadiness to find your way through.

KEY COMPONENTS: LINK TO THE ORIGINAL BROADCAST, EVOLUTIONARY LOVE CODES AND PRAYER

To supplement the written word, each episode includes a QR code linking to the original broadcast on YouTube, as well as occasional links to featured songs and video clips.

Each episode also centers around an "Evolutionary Love Code," formulated by Marc. These codes are part of the ongoing articulation and distillation of the *dharma* as it unfolds and emerges, week by week, over the course of many years, through the mystical process we call Outrageous Love or Evolutionary Love.

Another core component of the One Mountain, Many Paths episodes is what Marc and Barbara called "Evolutionary Prayer." Prayer is experienced in One Mountain not in the old fundamentalist sense of a "cosmic vending-machine god" who is alienated from Cosmos. Marc refers to this as the "god you do not and should not believe in"—and he often adds, "the god you don't believe in does not exist."

GOD IS THE INFINITE INTIMATE

In fact, in the *dharma* of CosmoErotic Humanism, a new name for God has emerged: the "Infinite Intimate," who appears in first-, second-, and third-person expressions. Marc first shared this name as he heard it whispered in 2023, although earlier intimations and formulations of the name appeared as early as 2010.

In first person, God is infinitely alive and as intimate as our own first-person experience.

In second person, God is the infinitely intimate Personhood of Cosmos that knows our name and holds us—the God about whom we say, whenever we fall, we fall into Her hands. This is the God who is our Beloved, Father, Mother, Lover, and Evolutionary Partner.

Finally, in third person, God inheres in all of the First Principles and First Values of Cosmos, and in the laws of science (both interior and exterior) that govern manifest Reality.

Therefore, we have a realization of God as not only the Infinity of Power but also the Infinity of Intimacy.

In One Mountain, Many Paths, we are reclaiming prayer at a higher level of consciousness. And we are reclaiming prayer as deep, alive, loving, and intimate conversations with God as the Infinite Intimate who knows our name.

THE INVITATION

We invite you to find your way into this revolution. Each one of our Unique Selves and unique gifts are desperately needed as we co-create this new Story of Value together, as part of the covenant between generations, for the sake of the whole.

Let's play a larger game and evolve the very source code of consciousness and culture together.

With mad love,

The Editors

LOVE OR DIE

LOCATING OURSELVES: ARTICULATING THE ESSENTIAL CONTEXT FOR THE ONE MOUNTAIN, MANY PATHS ORAL ESSAYS

SETTING OUR INTENTION

Intention setting is everything.

We're here—as da Vinci was with his cohort in the Renaissance—to play a larger game, to participate in the evolution of love, which is to tell the new Story of Value rooted in First Principles and First Values.

- Our intention is to recognize the critical historical juncture in which we find ourselves.
- Our intention is to take our seat at the table of history and to say, we take responsibility for this.
- Our intention is to participate as revolutionaries for the sake of the whole.

What we're here to do is revolution; revolution for the sake of the evolution of love.

It's a revolution for the sake of the trillions of unborn lives that will not manifest:

- The unborn loves
- The unborn creativity
- The unborn goodness
- The unborn truth
- The unborn beauty

All of it looks to us.

Not because we're engaged in grandiosity. Not at all!

- We're trembling before She.
- We're trembling with joy at the privilege.
- We're trembling with joy at the responsibility.
- We're trembling with joy at the Possibility of Possibility.
- We have to enact a new story in this moment of time. Because it is only a new story that can change the vector of history.

The most revolutionary act that we can do—the greatest moral imperative of this time—is to articulate a new story at this time between worlds and this time between stories.

Story is not made up, as postmodernity suggests. We all live in inescapable frameworks; our framework is the story we live in. Right now, Reality lives according to win/lose metrics, a story that is generating existential risk. We need to change that story.

When we change that story, when we tell a new story—not a made-up story, but a new Story of Value, rooted in First Principles and First Values—then it all changes.

We need to participate in the evolution of the source code of consciousness and culture, which is the evolution of love.

It's the most important, exciting, evolutionary, revolutionary act that we can do to alleviate suffering: to be lovers.

Like Rumi, the great poet of Sufism, we have to be "mad lovers," because it's the only sanity.

To be mad lovers is to see around the corner, to not be so obsessed with the details of the contractions of my life.

Let me see bigger.

Let me take complete care of myself in every possible way, let me completely attend to those in my circle of intimacy and influence, and then—let me expand my circle.

That's what we're here for.

- ◆ Our intention is to participate in the LoveForce, the LoveIntelligence, the LoveBeauty, the LoveDesire that literally animates Cosmos all the way up and all the way down.
- ◆ Our intention is to participate in the evolution of love.

[In the next few pages we will cover some key concepts which are essential to locating ourselves and setting the context for all the One Mountain, Many Paths Oral Essays. —Eds.]

OVERVIEW: EROS IS NO LONGER A LUXURY—IT'S LOVE OR DIE

Eros is life.

The failure of Eros destroys life.

Our lack of Eros is poised to destroy the world.

All civilizations have fallen because the stories that they lived in were, in some sense, stories based on rivalrous conflict governed by win/lose metrics. Every civilization was weakened by interior polarization caused by the lack of a shared Story of Value.

We now have a global civilization, but we haven't created a shared Story of Value.

We haven't solved the generator functions that caused all civilizations to fall. Our global civilization has exponential technologies and extraction models depleting the Earth of resources that took billions of years to create, which is going to lead to a civilizational collapse.

Existential risk is risk to our very existence.

The choice is clear: love or die.

It's that simple.

Eros is no longer a luxury. It is an absolute necessity for the survival of the individual and the planet.

In the last half a century, modern psychology has documented an age-old truth: a fully nourished baby who is not held in loving arms will die.

So too, our world, both personal and global—even with all the resources of intelligence and technology at our disposal—will die without being held in love, in the embrace of Eros.

We must embrace a personal path of love and a global politics of love.

Not ordinary love. Not love which is "mere human sentiment," but Eros, or what we sometimes call Outrageous Love, which is the heart of existence itself.

We live in a world of outrageous pain.

The only response is Outrageous Love.

WHAT IS EROS?

Eros is the experience of radical aliveness, moving towards, seeking, desiring ever deeper contact and ever greater wholeness.4 Eros is the core fabric of Reality's being and the motivational architecture of Reality's becoming.

Eros is what animates the evolutionary impulse itself, from the very inception of Cosmos all the way to our very selves, who awaken to the realization that the evolutionary impulse throbs uniquely in each of us.

The realization of human awakening and transformation that lies at the core of the interior sciences is the invitation—or even the urgent and desperate demand—of a madly loving Cosmos animated by infinities of power and infinities of intimacy.

The demand—the desperate invitation, the plea, the tender and fierce command of Cosmos that lives inside every human being—is to awaken: to awaken to our true nature as unique incarnations of Eros and Ethos that are needed and desperately desired by All-That-Is. Said slightly differently: Reality is Eros. Or: God is Eros.

The failure of Eros destroys life. The collapse of Eros is always the hidden (or not so hidden) root cause for the collapse of ethics.

This is true both personally and collectively. We live in a moment of a worldwide and personal collapse of Eros. Our lack of Eros is poised to destroy the world. Humanity is currently experiencing what has come to be known

---

4 We define Eros through what we refer to as the Eros equation (one of a series of what we call interior science equations):

Eros = Radical Aliveness x Desiring (Growing + Seeking) x Deeper Contact x Greater Wholeness x Self Actualization/Self Transcendence (Creation [Destruction])

There are good reasons for the formal language of the interior science equations in these writings, and the reader is invited to explore them on their own, in particular, in our work, David J. Temple, *First Principles and First Values: Forty-Two Propositions on CosmoErotic Humanism, the Meta-Crisis, and the World to Come* (World Philosophy and Religion, 2024).

as existential risk, a risk to our very existence, or what I will refer to as the Second Shock of Existence.

EXISTENTIAL RISK: THE SECOND SHOCK OF EXISTENCE

The first shock of existence is the death of the human being—the realization that we will die, which dawns in human consciousness at the beginning of history. We are not talking about the biological fact of death but the existential realization of death. Although the interior sciences disclose that death is a portal between two days (there is vast empirical,[5] philosophical,[6] and anthro-ontological evidence[7] for the continuity of consciousness[8]), death is also, in our own direct surface experience, a stark end. And that is obviously not a bug but a feature in the system.

---

5   We refer to evidence gathered by the most serious of researchers, beginning with Henry and Edith Sedgwick at Cambridge University and William James at Harvard University, and continuing in highly rigorous form for the last 150 years, as recapitulated by Whiteheadian scholar David Ray Griffin in multiple volumes. See also, for example, Dean Radin, *Real Magic: Unlocking Your Natural Psychic Abilities to Create Everyday Miracles* (Potter/TenSpeed/Harmony, 2018), *The Conscious Universe: The Scientific Truth of Psychic Phenomena* (HarperCollins, 2010), and other books. Or see the earlier classic by Frederic William Henry Myers, *Human Personality and Its Survival of Bodily Death* (Longmans, Green, 1907).

6   This requires a cogent analysis of materialism and dualism, and the introduction of the far more cogent third possibility which we have called "pan-interiority."

7   We discuss Anthro-Ontology in some depth in *First Principles and First Values*, and see also the fuller conversation in David J. Temple, *First Principles and First Values: Towards an Evolving Perennialism: Introducing the Anthro-Ontological Method*—both published by World Philosophy and Religion Press, in Conjunction with Integral Publishers. For now, we will simply define it as an "innate and clear interior gnosis directly available to the human being."

8 See Dr. Marc Gafni and Dr. Zachary Stein's essay in preparation, "Beyond Death: Anthro-Ontology, Philosophy, and Empiricism." This essay is slated to appear in the book *Towards a World Religion: Homo Amor Essays*. The essay is also the ground for a larger book by the same authors, *Twelve Portals to Life Beyond Death: Responding to the Second Shock of Existence,* in which we discuss three forms of material: the empirical, the philosophical, and the anthro-ontological, and show how each form discredits the notion of death as the end.

Our first-person experience is that death ends this life. It is not the totality of our experience if we go deeper inside, but it is obviously intended to be the central, potent, and painful dimension of every human life. Indeed, as Ernest Becker potently reminded us, the denial of death is at our peril.

All the stories and all the plotlines and all the threads of living end at that moment. Whatever happens beyond, we have an actual experience of ending. Paradoxically, that ending, the experience of the finality of mortality, is what presses us into life. From the implicit demand of the first shock of existence, human beings were activated and pressed into creative emergence, and what emerged was all of human culture, both interior and exterior.

The second shock of existence is the realization of the potential death of all humanity. After all the stages of human history—matter, life, and mind in all of their stages of evolutionary unfolding—we have come to this place in the evolution of humanity, in which the gap between our exponentially expanding exterior technologies and our stalled (or even regressing) interior technologies of value has created dire catastrophic and existential risks.

This gap generates extraction models and exponential growth curves, rivalrous conflicts based on win/lose metrics, tragedies of the commons, and multipolar traps, in which everyone has to keep producing to the nth degree, including weaponized exponential threats to our very existence because we are afraid that the other parties are going to do it and not be transparent—hide it from us and then dominate us.

GENERATOR FUNCTIONS FOR EXISTENTIAL RISK

Let's outline clearly the main generator functions for existential risk.

Rivalrous conflicts governed by zero-sum, win/lose metrics. Rivalrous conflicts generate extraction models at the core of the economic system and exponential growth curves. Both of these drive and are driven by a contrived system of artificially manufactured desires and needs, delivered into culture by ever more precise forms of micro-targeting to individuals and groups through the ever more immersive environment of the internet.

Next, rivalrous conflicts and exponential growth curves animated by win/lose metrics generate complicated, fragile world systems highly vulnerable to myriad forms of collapse. Fragile local systems are made exponentially more fragile on a global level by our inability to meet global challenges with social, legal, political, economic, and ethical infrastructures that remain largely local.

All of this is a direct result of the failure to develop more adequate interior technologies that would be sufficiently compelling to displace "rivalrous conflict governed by win/lose metrics" as the motivational architecture for the human life world.

This failure has led to the conditions that will cause the implosion of systems that are already and quite literally on the brink of collapsing themselves. That's what we mean by the second shock of existence.

To recapitulate: the second shock of existence is not the death of the human being, but the potential death of humanity.

It is the Death Star moment of our species.

THE DECONSTRUCTION OF INTRINSIC VALUE

We stand in this moment poised between utopia and dystopia, at a time between worlds and a time between stories. We need a new Story of Value, eternal yet evolving, rooted in First Principles and First Values, which would become a universal grammar of value and a context for our diversity.

This is exactly what the Renaissance was. It was a time between worlds and a time between stories. In the Renaissance, we had been recently challenged by the Black Death, a pandemic that swept across Europe. The Black Death destroyed between a third to half of Europe and a huge part of Asia. People died horrifically, brutally, in the streets. They had no idea how to meet this challenge, and so, in response to the Black Death, da Vinci and Ficino and their cohorts understood that they had to tell a new Story of Value.

That story was the story of modernity. Did they get it right?

- They got part of it right, which birthed, to use Jürgen Habermas' phrase, "the dignities of modernity," such as new ways of gathering information and universal human rights.
- But they also deconstructed the source of Value. They lost the basis for the Good, the True, and the Beautiful.

The basis used to be divine revelation: God told us. But this claim was owned by religion, and every religion began to overreach and over-claim. The revelation was thus often mediated through cultural categories and wasn't fully accurate.

Modernity threw out revelation, but was unable to establish a new basis for value.

Value was just assumed to be real. As it says in the founding document of the American Revolution: We hold these truths to be self-evident—that is, we don't really have a basis for value; we just take it as a given.

In other words, modernity took out a loan of social capital from the traditional world. The source of value was never worked out.

And then, gradually, value began to collapse.

- The Universe Story began to collapse.
- The belief that the Good, the True, and the Beautiful are real began to collapse.
- The belief that Love is real began to collapse.

As Bertrand Russell is reported to have said, "I cannot see how to refute the arguments for the subjectivity of ethical values, but I find myself incapable of believing that all that is wrong with wanton cruelty is that I do not like it."

What do you do if you grew up in a world in which value is not real? A world without a source of value, without a Universe Story, without a story of human identity, without a story of desire, without a narrative of power?

In the words of W.B. Yeats, the center does not hold.

- You have a collapse at the very center of society, because you no longer have Eros.
- You no longer have a Reality in which value is real, and so you have this lingering sense of emptiness.
- You have a complete collapse at the very center.
- We become the hollow men and the stuffed men, gesture without form.

And that's the source of our current existential risk.

THE DEEPER ROOT CAUSE OF THE META-CRISIS: A GLOBAL INTIMACY DISORDER

Above, I have outlined the major generator functions of existential risk. But there is a deeper cause for the existential risk that lurks underneath the rivalrous conflict governed by win/lose metrics and the fragile systems they engender.

And we cannot take the Death Star down without discerning and addressing this. We have already alluded to this root cause above, but at this point we need to make it more explicit so that, from this context, the adequate root response will become clear.

Modernity threw out the revelation, but was unable to establish a new basis for value.

This ostensibly surprising statement can be understood in a few simple steps:

- All of the catastrophic and existential risk challenges we face are global: from climate change to artificial intelligence, pandemics, systems collapse, and exponential arms races.
- Every global challenge self-evidently requires a global solution.
- Global solutions can only be implemented with global co-ordination.
- Global co-ordination is impossible without global coherence.
- Global coherence is only possible if there is a global resonance between the parts.
- Global resonance is only possible if we have global intimacy.

ONLY A SHARED STORY OF VALUE CAN GENERATE GLOBAL INTIMACY

Global intimacy—just like intimacy in a couple—is only possible when there is a shared story.

Not just a shared history, but a shared Story of Value.

- It is only a shared global story that can generate a new emergent quality of intimacy: global intimacy.
- A shared Story of Value must be rooted in shared ordinating values, or what we have called evolving First Values and First Principles.
- Intimacy requires a shared grammar of value as a matrix for a shared Story of Value.

The global intimacy disorder is the root cause for existential risk. The global intimacy disorder underlies the core generator functions for existential risk.

The global intimacy disorder is rooted in the failure to experience ourselves in a field of shared intrinsic value. This failure derives from the deconstruction of value.

Indeed, it is wholly accurate to say that the root cause of the two generator functions of existential risk is the failed story of intrinsic value, or what we might also call the breakdown of Eros.

- The first generator function is the success story. Our modern success story is rivalrous conflict governed by win/lose metrics, which violates all the terms of the Intimacy Equation: there is no shared identity and no mutuality of recognition, feeling, value or purpose, and instead of relative otherness, there is alienated otherness. Such a story generates complicated fragile systems with no allurement or intimacy between the parts, systems which optimize for efficiency (as an expression of win/lose metrics) and not for resiliency and life.

- The second generator function is the deconstruction of intrinsic value itself. The deconstruction of value is the sense that human value does not participate in the intrinsic value of the Real, for the Real is dogmatically declared to have no intrinsic value. Thus, there is no shared identity between the interior of the human being and Reality. There is no common participation in a field of shared intrinsic value. Instead of being intimate with value, we are alienated from value. And only intrinsic value can arouse will: political, moral, and social will.

To sum up, without a shared grammar of value there is no global intimacy, and therefore no global coherence, and no global coordination in response to catastrophic and existential risk, which means, put simply, there will be, quite literally, no future.

HEALING THE GLOBAL INTIMACY DISORDER
REQUIRES THE EVOLUTION OF INTIMACY

But we are not hopeless. On the contrary, we are filled with great hope. Hope is a memory of the future. That memory of the future is the direct hit that takes down the Death Star, the culture of death. The direct hit must be—as it has always been in history—the emergence of a new stage of evolution.

Crisis is an evolutionary driver, and every crisis is, at its core, a crisis of intimacy: from the oxygen crisis of the single cells dying which generated multicellular life at the dawn of existence, to the existential risk in this very moment.9

> *The direct hit is therefore structurally self-evident: the evolution of intimacy itself.*

What is intimacy, as a structure of Cosmos all the way down and all the way up the evolutionary chain? We engage this inquiry in depth in other writings, but for now we will simply adduce what we have called the "Intimacy Equation":

Intimacy = shared identity in the context of [relative] otherness x mutuality of recognition x mutuality of pathos x mutuality of value x mutuality of purpose

Intimacy is about the capacity of parts to generate a shared identity while retaining their otherness, or distinct identity. This requires multiple mutualities, including recognition, pathos (or feeling), value, and purpose. The parts must recognize and feel each other, even as they share value and

---

9 We demonstrate this principle in some depth in the multi-volume series, *The Universe: A Love Story* (forthcoming) (https://worldphilosophyandreligion.org/early-ontologies), *The Intimate Universe: Global Intimacy Disorder as Cause for Global Action Paralysis* (forthcoming), and in other writings of CosmoErotic Humanism.

purpose. But all of this must lead to intimate union—and not pathological fusion, where the distinct identity of the parts disappears—like subatomic particles that successfully become an atom, or two people who successfully become a couple.

THE DECONSTRUCTION OF VALUE IS THE DECONSTRUCTION OF INTIMACY

We have identified the global intimacy disorder as the root cause of the existential risk. But the underlying ultimate failure of intimacy is the deconstruction of value itself.

The deconstruction of value means that human value does not participate in any sense of intrinsic value of the Real. This is not about individual values, but about the Field of Value that underlies all of them. When the human being—moved, often sincerely or even nobly, by myriad cultural, historical, and psychological confusions—claims to have stepped out of the Field of Value, then intimacy itself is deconstructed.

The deconstruction of value is the deconstruction of intimacy.

In the absence of a shared Story of Value, a story that is an authentic expression of Reality's Eros, a story rooted in pseudo-Eros takes center stage and becomes the generator function for existential risk. Our modern pseudo-Eros story is rivalrous conflict governed by win/lose metrics. Such a story catalyzes in its wake the second generator function of existential risk: complicated fragile systems with no allurement or intimacy between the parts. It is in that sense that we have argued that the first generator function for existential risk is the success story.

- The failure of intimacy is precisely the impotent experience that there is no shared identity between the interior of the human being and Reality. There is no shared identity in the sense of any kind of common participation in a field of shared intrinsic value.

- But only a shared Story of Value can arouse the global will required to engage catastrophic and existential risk. For it is only global political, moral, and social will—and we can even say erotic will—that can generate the most Good, True and Beautiful world that we have always known is possible.

THE EVOLUTION OF LOVE IS THE TELLING OF A NEW STORY

Coupled with the Intimacy Equation is the scientifically grounded realization, in both the exterior and interior sciences, that Reality is a progressive deepening of intimacies, or, said slightly differently:

Reality is Evolution. Evolution is the evolution of intimacy.

- The evolution of intimacy requires—both personally and collectively—a deeper, more accurate discernment of the nature of our universe, ourselves, and our beloveds.
- This new discernment generates a new global Story of Value.
- The new global Story of Value generates an emergent, heretofore unseen global intimacy and heals the global intimacy disorder.

The new Story of Value is the direct hit that takes down the Death Star and replaces it with the hope that invokes the memory of our best future.

Global intimacy facilitates global coherence, which facilitates global co-ordination, which activates the possibility of our creative and effectively coordinated global responses to the global meta-crisis in its entirety and its specific expressions.

To solve Bertrand Russell's challenge—the apparent argument for the subjectivity of ethical values—we have to reground value theory in eternal yet evolving First Principles and First Values, and articulate a new Story of Value.

This is what we call CosmoErotic Humanism.

CosmoErotic Humanism—together with other emergent strands—needs to become the ground of a world religion as a context for our diversity. We need religion, even as we need science, to articulate a shared global grammar of value.

As we said at the beginning, our choice is simple: love or die.

- To love means to participate in the evolution of love, which is the evolution of the human Story of Value.
- To love means to evolve and activate a new cultural enlightenment—rooted in a new narrative of identity, a new narrative of value, a new narrative of intimate communion, a new narrative of desire, a new narrative of power—all of which will birth new narratives of economics and politics.
- The evolution of love is the telling of a new story.

The new story that must be told is a love story, for in fact that is the deepest truth of Reality, rooted in the best exterior and interior sciences, that we have at this moment in time:

- Reality is not merely a fact. Reality is a story.
- Reality is not an ordinary story. Reality is a love story.
- Reality is not an ordinary love story. Reality is an Outrageous Love Story.

Story doesn't mean it's made-up.

It means doing the hard work of integrating the validated insights of the traditional world, the modern world, and the postmodern world.

This is the intention at the heart of telling the new Story of CosmoErotic Humanism.

ABOUT THIS VOLUME

What do we mean when we say we are an *Evolutionary Church* practicing *Evolutionary Love*?

In Evolutionary Church we are reclaiming love as a religion. We're not reclaiming a religion of love. We're actually reclaiming *love as a religion*. We are the One-World Church, telling the new Universe Story through a new Gospel. So the purpose of the church is to reclaim (for the first time in history), not the religion of love, but love as a religion.

And it's not just love but *evolving* love, Evolutionary Love. Love not only as a static, eternal constant, but love that is the Eros Value of all of Reality, grounded in eternity and yet ever evolving.

In this new Universe Story, Evolutionary Love is the animating Eros of Cosmos. The One-World Church becomes the institutionalization of a new politics of love, a new religion of love, a new science of love, and a new psychology of love, guided by the realization that eternal and evolving Evolutionary Love is the heart of existence itself.

In Evolutionary Love, "evolutionary" of course means evolving, moving towards a more refined, more complex, more conscious, and more loving state. Evolutionary love, however, is not only a third-person force that drives forward evolution. We are not only products of evolution. We do not only live in a world that is evolving.

We not only live in evolution. Evolution lives in us.

Evolutionary Love lives in us. We participate in the real—in Reality—as unique expressions of Evolutionary Love. We are the evolutionary impulse in person; we are the personal face of Evolutionary Love.

As *Homo amor*, we recognize Evolutionary Love as being the animating force of Reality.

We recognize ourselves as *Homo amor, the fulfillment of Homo sapiens*. We are Evolutionary Love in person.

As *Homo amor*:

- We experience our personal and communal love as participating in Evolutionary Love.
- We recognize Reality as being an Evolutionary Love Story.
- We recognize that we participate in the Evolutionary Love Story of Reality.
- We recognize that our love story is chapter and verse in *The Universe: A Love Story.*

We evolve our understanding of what it means to be human, and what it means to love. We evolve our understanding of the nature of Reality, the nature of relationship, the nature of religion, of gender, of story, and of God.

We become intimate with Reality in a new way.

We recognize that *we live in an Intimate Universe, and that the Intimate Universe lives in us.*

We recognize that Reality, God, is the Infinity of Intimacy.

God is the Infinite Intimate.

We recognize that evolution is the evolution of intimacy, and that we participate in that evolution.

In the new story of CosmoErotic Humanism, we have articulated an intimacy equation in which intimacy is formulated as:

Intimacy is shared identity in the context of relative otherness and a mutuality of recognition, feeling, value and purpose.

In this sense, we understand that the evolution of intimacy is the evolution of this shared identity. As such, we evolve intimacy by expanding our shared identity and ultimately becoming intimate with all of Reality.

As we evolve our intimacy from egocentric to ethnocentric to worldcentric to cosmocentric intimacy, our moral community expands to include all of Reality.

- Egocentric intimacy means care and concern—willingness to sacrifice and radical commitment—for my circle of family and close friends, my survival clan.
- Ethnocentric intimacy means an expansion of care and concern—willingness to sacrifice and radical commitment—for my entire tribe, nation, or religion; my larger sociocentric or ethnocentric community.
- Worldcentric intimacy means an expansion of care and concern—willingness to sacrifice and radical commitment—for every person on the planet.
- Cosmocentric intimacy means an expansion of care and concern—willingness to sacrifice and radical commitment—not only for every human being, but for every animal, for the earth, the Universe and even the Cosmos: past, present, and future.

As the intimacy equation shows, we evolve our intimacy in the *context of otherness*. Intimacy does not erase uniqueness. Just the opposite. Indeed, our irreducible uniqueness can only be fully expressed in the depth of intimacy. Within the depth of radical intimacy, we can experience the full expression of our uniqueness.

Each human being is a unique word in the cosmic scroll. Each word is composed of distinct letters. Each letter is a different voice that lives the person. Integrated together, those different voices constitute the unique word, the unique quality of intimacy, and the unique purpose of that person's word in the Universe: A Love Story."

We recognize that we are each irreducibly unique configurations of intimacy and that our uniqueness is desperately needed by all of Reality.

Finally, we realize that the evolution of intimacy—as it takes shape in the unique contours of our unique lives—participates directly in the evolution of God as the Infinity of Intimacy itself. In other words, the evolution of our intimacy is participatory in the evolution of the Intimate Universe.

Volume 15

These oral essays are edited talks delivered by Marc Gafni and Barbara Marx Hubbard between June and August 2019.

CHAPTER ONE

PARTICIPATING IN THE EVOLUTION OF RELIGION AND GOD VISION

Episode 141 — June 22, 2019

WE NEED A SHARED STORY OF *DHARMA*

What's the core intention of church? A bunch of years ago, I started something called the Center for World Spirituality. We then changed it into the Center for Integral Wisdom with Sally Kempton, Ken Wilber, Mariana Caplan, Zak Stein, and a whole host of other luminaries. We had this vision then of articulating *what a world spirituality might look like*, and as the next step, *what a world religion might look like*? Imagine that for a second.

There's a long conversation I had with a gentleman named Michael Murphy, who founded Esalen and is the owner of Esalen, and one of the godfathers of the human potential movement. Michael and I had many dinners for a period of time.

I said to Michael, *the problem with Esalen is there's no dharma; there's no uniting story. Everyone does what they do, everyone is honored in their beautiful track, but there's no shared story. It's like Esalen is rebelling against dogmatic narratives from an earlier time.*

Therefore, as Michael said to me, *no one can capture the flag; any teacher does whatever they want.*

It's very beautiful for individual experiences, and that rebellion against dogmatic narratives is really important, but that's not where we are today. **Actually, we're at a moment today where we need a shared story.** Not a dogmatic story, not an imposed story. Not a story where some group says, *we own it and you don't have it.* He correctly rebelled against that.

We need a shared story, not of dogma, but of dharma.

What does *dharma* mean? We're using the word *dharma* in the Evolutionary Church. It's why Barbara came and stood together with us. When Barbara and I met, we exploded together with this idea of there being a new *dharma*. Barbara called me a week before she died, and she said, *the last four years of my life have been the most exciting years of my life, we're formulating a dharma.* Meaning, we're taking the best insights of the interior sciences and the exterior sciences, lined with love, and we're telling a new story. That new story is after postmodernity deconstructed everything. We are the reconstructive project for *what the shared story is.*

Now, you know why this matters? Because without a shared story, we're actually not going to make it in this 11th hour. **We're not going to make it across this 11th hour unless there's a shared story of identity, a shared story of community, a shared Universe Story. And that's got to articulate itself in this new** *dharma.*

We are in revolution here, but it's a sacred revolution. We're reclaiming a *dharma* that is that *there's a shared* story. Religion, from *religare*, means to connect; to have vision of the patterns that connect, to have a vision of a new Universe Story. Because when there's no new Universe Story, we can't make it. Our kids need to know what their identity is. Our kids need to have a sense of *where they're located, and their narrative of identity.* The reason kids are failing to launch is because they don't know how to answer the question: *who am I?*

Look at what happens when people don't know who they are:

- There's the opioid crisis.
- There are 25 million attempted suicides around the world each year.
- In the United States, every few days, someone shoots up a school and no one even notices.

What happened? We actually lost touch with our core identity. *What makes us noble beings? Where's our nobility? Where's our duty? Where's our honor? Where's our sacred obligation that wells up from within us?*

Without a shared narrative of identity, we don't have coherence. Barbara and I, literally in the days before she died, we talked about coherence. What does it mean to cohere? We can cohere only if we're living in a shared story, not a dogmatic story owned by one religion, but a new world spirituality.

RECLAIMING LOVE AS RELIGION IN WHICH OUR MORAL COMMUNITY IS ALL OF REALITY

I want to use a hard word for a second, it's a little bit of a polarizing word. But it's good that it's polarizing because it actually wakes us up. It's electric. So if you will, we begin to vision what it would mean to claim a world religion. Now in that world religion, none of the religions disappear, but they evolve. **A world religion is a shared framework in which you get to be a dual citizen; you can be Jewish or Buddhist or Taoist or Confucius,**

or any frame of Islam or any kind of Christianity. But there's also a shared world religion in which we're all part of at least a world framework or a world spirituality.

Imagine the *chutzpah* of saying, *We're actually going to declare a world religion; we're going to actually formulate what a world religion would look like.* Not that we're owning it. It's not the old notion of *we're the priests and we own it.* It's a world in which every person is a priest and priestess, every person is a God and Goddess; every person is a Unique Self.

I had a deep conversation yesterday. We've been talking about Outrageous Love, and we've talked about the church of Evolutionary Love. What are we really saying? What's the core mission of our church? In the church, what we're saying is, we're not reclaiming a religion of love—that went bad with Christianity. We're actually *reclaiming love as a religion.* That's what *Homo amor* means: *amor*, love. Remember King Solomon, who said, *its insides are lined with love.* But Solomon didn't yet have evolution and the evolutionary story.

The evolutionary story says that it is Eros or love that actually animates all the four forces of Reality: the electromagnetic, the nuclear, the strong and the weak. It's all animated by love. Its insides are lined with love. Charles Sanders Peirce, the greatest evolutionary theorist, says, *Evolutionary Love drives the whole story.* I was privileged that Ken Wilber and I wrote an essay on that eight or nine years ago.

That's why Barbara stood with us. Barbara called me and said: *Marc, I want to stand with you. I'm 84 years old, I've spoken to everyone and I've been everywhere, but we need to go the next step. I'm reading what you all are doing, and I'm reading Evolutionary Love and the evolution of intimacy.*

The evolution of intimacy equals the evolution of *shared identity in the context of otherness*. What does that sentence mean? It means intimacy is shared identity; molecules come together to form complex molecules, quarks come together to form an atom, and atoms form a molecule.

4

That's a shared identity. But then we evolve intimacy by expanding our shared community and forming new identities. In the Evolutionary Church, when we're actually part of the same identity, we form a shared identity in the context of otherness; we never lose our uniqueness.

Imagine this for a second. I want to give you a sense of what we're doing here. The evolution of intimacy means *my shared identity expands*. Here's the big sentence: we need to know that our moral community is all of Reality.

The most important thing to do, at this moment between utopia and dystopia, is to realize that my moral community is actually all of planet Earth.

Love and the evolution of love—it's not just love; love has become a very bland word—moving love from egocentric to ethnocentric to world centric to cosmocentric, expanding my identity, being intimate with the whole story.

That means I feel the pain of the whole story, and I feel the joy of the whole story. Just as I'm committed to feed myself when I'm hungry, I'm committed to stand in the abyss between dystopia and utopia and give my unique gift and say: *Let there be light*. Because I'm intimate with Reality.

It's not a job. It's not even a vocation—**it's my very identity.**

What are we here to say? We're here to say that we're not reestablishing the religion of love. No. The purpose of the church is to reclaim (for the first time in history), not the religion of love, **but love as a religion.**

Each one of us has unique expressions of LoveIntelligence coming together in a Unique Self Symphony.

GOD IS THE INFINITY OF POWER AND THE INFINITY OF INTIMACY

Friends, we move into prayer. We move into prayer, and what do we do? One of the things we're doing in church is, it's literally an Outrageous Love revolution.

By Outrageous Love, we mean love is a religion.

Remember, love has gotten very pallid. We say, *I love you,* so easily. *When words lose their meaning, culture collapses.* By love, we mean Evolutionary Love, Outrageous Love; the love that drives all of Cosmos, the love that's *not mere human sentiment but the heart of existence itself.*

That love is not opposed to power. Jimi Hendrix got a lot of things right, and he did *The Star-Spangled Banner* way back in the 60s at Woodstock, but he got one thing wrong. He said, *The world is going to get better when the power of love is greater than the love of power.* Jimmy, I love you madly, brother, and you lived a gorgeous life, flaming till age 27. But you got that one wrong, brother. Love and power are not opposed to each other; love and power are actually inextricably combined.

Love is the power that animates and drives Reality. *I am a unique expression* of the evolutionary impulse. That means *I am love in action. And power blows through me and moves through me.*

When we split off our power, it goes underground and comes out as abuse.

That's why when we talk about *amor, amor* is filled with power—but *power for the sake of.* When we hold *power over,* we hold it with such gentleness and with such tenderness, because we all have power over each other. There's no one who doesn't have power over someone, and someone has power over us. We love surrendering to the trust of a person actually activating their power. When you love someone, you give them power.

We turn to the Divine face in prayer, who is not this powerful God in this negative, weird, dystopian, angry God-in-the-sky sense, but rather what we call the second face of God: God who's the Infinity of Intimacy. God who is the Infinity of Intimacy is also the Infinity of Power.

Just as in us, love and power are not split, in divinity love and power are not split. God is the Infinity of Intimacy and the Infinity of Power.

God, who is inherent to Cosmos, who both holds us from without, and lives in us and embraces us and hears every word, God is our Outrageous Lover; God is our intimate Beloved. That's what the Song of Solomon is all about. That's what pseudo-Dionysius is all about. That's what Evolutionary Love is all about. God says: *Tell me everything, tell me about your holy and your broken Hallelujah.*

We come to pray. For Barbara, this was literally her favorite part of the church. Barbara used to say to me, in the last two years, every day she'd write, and she say, *I grew up and my father said, "You're American, and your religion is to be successful." I never knew what prayer was, I thought prayer was just the fundamentalists.*

We need to reclaim words like prayer. When I started talking about prayer 10–20 years ago in the human potential movement, people cringed. But actually, we have to reclaim prayer. We can't live in our silo, our bubble. 75% of the world lives in a world religion, and the liberal progressive world is dissociated from the larger context.

Actually, prayer is beautiful. But what does prayer mean? Prayer is not prayer to an ethnocentric, homophobic God who tells you that you're going to go to hell for breaking this law or that law. No. Prayer is when we turn to God who is the Infinity of Intimacy. Prayer affirms the dignity of personal need.

I want to invite everyone to do a little meditation with me. Shut your eyes and imagine what we call here, God in the third person: the infinite laws of complexity and physics, and they're mapped by complexity theory. The mathematics of all of manifest Reality, hundreds of billions and billions of light years and universes and multiverses and exponential expanded elegance and complexity beyond any and all imagination. All of God in the third-person, vast infinite power over vast infinite time. All of that is now sitting in a chair right next to you, looking at you—God in the second-person—loving you madly, hearing every word that you speak, and wanting to know everything as your Outrageous Lover. Because feel this for a second, where did you come from? Reality manifested you. It manifested you uniquely and loves you madly. That's not a dogma. That's an interior realization. That's *dharma*.

We turn to God/Goddess, who is both within us and also beyond us. Rumi fell into Her arms when Rumi prayed. We turn to the Infinity of Intimacy as we reclaim prayer at a higher level of consciousness. And what do we do? We ask for everything. Dharma is love. We reclaim prayer and ask for everything. We are in Florence now. We are da Vinci in Florence, and we are standing at the abyss of the Black Death. We're standing and saying we're going to tell a new story, like da Vinci did, which brought in modernity. Now we're going to tell a new story which is actually going to take us to the next level.

This new story is the minor fluctuation point in systems theory that jumps the entire system to a higher order.

WE ARE UNIQUE MEMBERS OF A LIVING BODY

Evolutionary Love Code:

> There's a corner of the world that is unloved. That corner of the world waits for you to give your unique gifts of LoveIntelligence and LoveBeauty.

> If you do not do so, your life will have failed. If you do so, you will have a life of grand success.

No one other than you knows your unique gift that is yours to give, and no one will call you out other than Reality itself.

So, there's a corner of the world that's unloved that needs me, that needs you, that needs us. Let's penetrate into the revelation of what we're saying about the world when we say this. What we're discovering in the Evolutionary Church, and in understanding the story of evolution as our own story, is that the world is a living system. It's alive, all of it. That this world that we are now part of is at the exact phase of its own evolution. It's like a birth, where this world itself can go into devolution and destruction very easily, but it is calling for the evolution of this world through us. That's how the world is going to evolve.

If you get in touch with the uniqueness of yourself, and your LoveIntelligence and LoveBeauty, and take it for granted that there is a place where it fits best, because the world is a living system. Just like we have eye cells and ear cells, we have trillions of cells creating a physical body.

How many cells together, doing what they need to do best, will it take to form a new world?

That's really our question. When we talk about the politics of love, it's not only generalized love. It's the love of everybody giving their uniqueness at the place where it fits best into the social body, until the entire social body comes alive.

How do we do this? Well, in the famous phrase of evolution, you only do it in the muddy pools of evolution. You don't come out of the sea as a fish and suddenly get on the Empire State Building to say, *I'm a human*. You go through lots and lots of phases to get to the next step.

The phase that we're in right now is we're in a planetary crisis of birth. It's dangerous, and that's not in any way underestimating the pain of the birth. But you can't get through this birth unless you see that you're being born.

In the Evolutionary Church, we are seeing ourselves being born as unique members of a living body that is itself coming alive in a universe

9

probably filled with life, wherein every one of us is going to go the whole way. We are declaring in this church that we're going to go the whole way in this lifetime. Because you know what? We don't have time to go the whole way two lifetimes from now.

We're the lucky generation that's born in exactly the moment of the planetary birth. That's why we're feeling the pain of all the things that are not working, and we're also feeling the passion and joy to give our gift.

BECOMING PARTNERS WITH EACH OTHER IN THIS EVOLUTIONARY COMMUNITY

I want to say something about the feeling of being able to give your gift, and define the community that needs what you have to give, and you need to receive what others have to give to you. Let's realize that if there's any deep meaning of social joy and personal joy in life, it's finding that. It's like Pierre Teilhard de Chardin says: *Tap, tap, tap like a blind person*, because you don't fully know where you're needed.

But here's the good news. I think we who are in this evolutionary community—not only in this church but anywhere in the world—are finding where we are needed—and where we fit best. That means if you could look at the Earth from space and see something light up somewhere in this communication system of the planetary body, you would see people turn on like this. You would see people going to the places where they need to go. You would see centers of awakening in the planetary body—that is you and me right now. We're all on the internet. I'm a little hologram coming to you. It's truly stunning if you just think of it, this is awesome! **If we lived at the time of Jesus Christ, they'd think we were all gods**. We're traveling like this—we're going anywhere, everywhere, simultaneously, where we fit best.

I'd like everybody to get deeply in touch with your unique greatness and your unique LoveBeauty, as a member of this evolutionary community, thinking of it as something that has been convened by us to be a demonstration of what this can be. I feel that as we develop this church, and as we learn to come together physically as well as on the internet, and as we read each other's writings, there's a huge evolutionary code going on here. There's a huge story of creation being revealed to us. **We are the pioneers of the next stage of evolution, joined together right now, right here.**

Just last night, I went to see a movie called *The Darkest Hour* about Churchill. It somehow reminded me a lot about some of us because Churchill, first of all, was considered eccentric. He was not even very well-liked by most of the members of parliament when he was chosen. But the reason he had to be chosen is that the situation was that Hitler was running over Europe, and Hitler was revealing his cruelty, his viciousness and his awesome terror.

The people in the Parliament of Great Britain were saying, *let's make peace.* Chamberlain was saying that, most of them were saying that, and Churchill was finally called in because nobody knew what to do.

> Here's a horror. We want to make peace; we don't want to fight.
> It's much more intelligent not to fight.

And Churchill gets in there, as he's smoking a cigar and drinking his brandy in the morning.

He intuitively knows that they have to fight. He has to send men to Calais so that the Dunkirk can be evacuated, and these men are going to be killed. The sophisticated people said, *don't send those men, they'll be killed.*

He said, *Well good, we're going to be killed totally unless we do this.* As he moves forward, he doubts himself. Is it right to fight back? We're not talking about fighting here that we have to do, but he did have to do that. There are times when we have to fight back.

He finally attracted the king, and the king came in late in the evening. Churchill is sitting on his bed depressed about whether he's doing the wrong thing. The king sits next to Churchill in this movie and he says, *I'm your partner.* And with that, Churchill was empowered. **We need to say** that to each other: *I'm your partner.* I'd like to say, *I'm your partner here in this church.* I'm here for you 100%. You're here for me and for each other.

Then what happened was, Churchill got up there at the Parliament, and there's Chamberlain and there are the people who said, *Let's make peace.* Meanwhile, there's this horror of Hitler. The United States wouldn't come in, Roosevelt wouldn't come in—nobody would come in. Churchill stood there, and with that one thing that he had—the king who came and gave him partnership—he said, *Never give in! Never, never, never!* He launched the Battle of Britain, and the entire parliament went wild with joy. The people of Great Britain decided they would be the greatest people on Earth.

Somebody said, *How did Churchill do this?* One of the remarks, which I love because it reminds me of Marc Gafni, is they said, *Well, he mobilized the English language to do it.* That is to say, he had the words; he had the force, he had the voice, he had the creativity. In so doing, he mobilized Great Britain, who saved the world. Finally, we came in when we were attacked by Japan.

We find ourselves now facing, not a Hitler, but a life threat of many kinds, and we are the partners who say: *Yes, we have the power, we have the greatness, we have the vision, and we're heading for a planetary awakening in love through a unique synergistic symphony.*

WORLD SPIRITUALITY IS RECLAIMING AND UPLEVELING RELIGION

Amen! Let's pick up this word, and let's look at our code together. *There's a corner of the world that is unloved.* The King is sitting next to you, and the King is saying, *I am your partner.* To actually create this new vision, this new world spirituality, to reclaim religion. Feel the cringe in your body when you say the word religion; we feel all the old words, we feel all of the corruption, we feel all of the tragedy. Voltaire said, *Remember the cruelties.* Yet what happens is we forget that we have to actually reclaim the original impulse—*re-ligare*—and that we have to actually up-level prayer.

The word *God*, for a huge part of the progressive world today, is a word you can't use. But we actually use the word here because we're up-leveling, we're participating as God in the evolution of God; we're *religaring*. **We're declaring the possibility of a world religion and a world spirituality, in which every religion shines, in which every possibility shines—a genuine pluralism**. We're part of a larger story. It's the new story. It is the realization of *amor*. Not the religion of love, but Outrageous Love—love as Outrageous Love, as Evolutionary Love, as religion, as Spirit, as Goodness, as Truth, as Beauty.

The King stands next to us and sits next to us, and the King says, *you can do this*. Can we just say to each other: *I'm the King, I'm your partner*. Because we're all the King. The King is beyond us and holding us, the Infinity of Intimacy right now. But we're also saying it to each other, *You can do this. I'm the queen, I'm your partner. I'm the king, I am your partner*. Let's feel it. Can we say to each other even when we're closed, *you can do this*? Sometimes, we get stuck with each other—we get stuck on being right.

I had a hard morning. I woke up late. I got in very late last night, so I slept for about five hours. There was a really important text that I received that I needed to respond to. When the person sent the text that said, *Why didn't you respond to my text*? I said, *Oh my God, I texted you five times yesterday*. Then this person said to me, *What do you mean you texted me yesterday? Today is today*! Sometimes we just say, *Wow, I missed something, I'm so sorry I missed it.*

Let's all forgive each other, love each other so madly, and turn to each other and say: *You can do this*. We have to always forgive each other; we're all imperfect vessels for the light. *But you can do this*. Now let's bring it from 'you' to 'we.' Can it be: *We can do this? We can do this*! That's the realization. Love as spirit. Love as religion. Yes, I feel the same thing in my body; *religion, arghh!* But actually, 60–70 percent of the world lives under a religion, and the movement to take down the World Trade Centre in New York was a movement of religion. We need to take down bad, premodern, shadowy religion.

But we can't move beyond religion, we have to up-level the religion. The same way we can't move beyond God. We have to actually participate in the evolution of God and the evolution of religion. In this religion, everyone has a place. It could be the religion of atheism, but we're *religaring*—we're reconnecting. Atheism says, *I can't get into that old theism thing, but I get Evolutionary Love.* We can do anything together. Just feel that. Our question always is, *I want to know what love is.* Let's do that prayer together. Let's know that that's love as religion. Barbara, this is our vision together.

We think that there's someone else that's going to do it somewhere—and I have tears in my eyes now—we think there's some room where it's happening, but *this is ours to do.* We can do this! Barbara, we're partnering with you, evolutionary partner.

> And we forgive each other.
> And we meet each other.
> And we find each other.
> And we're each other's king.

As Barbara said, we sit next to each other on the bed when there's no one around, and we say, *I'm your partner, I can do this with you.* We're all going to make mistakes, but we're in and we can do this. Loving each other madly! We're between utopia and dystopia. The church of Evolutionary Love, One Church, we're doing this together.

We can do this!

CHAPTER TWO

NOT THE RELIGION OF LOVE, BUT LOVE AS RELIGION

Episode 142 — June 29, 2019

THIS IS LOVE AS RELIGION

Our intention is to be the One Church—not the only church, but the One Church that includes all churches and all synagogues and all mosques. But we need to be one church, and we call ourselves One Church because that which unites us is so much greater than that which divides us. And we need to begin to tell the story of a shared humanity. It's one world. It's one church. And **we need to move beyond polarization**.

As we stand in this moment, facing existential risk of the kind that Reality has never known, what will allow us to respond to existential risk, which at its core we understand to be a global intimacy disorder? What we need to do is restore intimacy, and we restore intimacy through restoring, reclaiming, and evolving the emergent shared story:

- ◆ The shared narrative of identity: the answer to the question of *who am I?*
- ◆ The shared narrative of We: the answer to the question of *who are we?*
- ◆ The shared understanding that *amor*, that love itself, in its most core and beautiful way, stands at the core of everything.

This is not the religion of love. The religion of love, in many ways, was a tragedy. Christianity in so many ways made a contribution, and in so many other ways went corrupt, so tragically. It's why when Voltaire ushered in the new enlightenment, the French Enlightenment, he said, *Remember the cruelties.*

This is not the religion of love. This is love as religion.

By religion, we mean *religare*. Religion means there's a shared code. But it's not a shared code that's imposed from without. It's not a tyrannical code. It's *dharma*. It's a shared vision. It's a shared narrative of identity, in which we understand that we are each of us *Homo amor*; we are each of us unique configurations of the LoveIntelligence and LoveBeauty. What would it mean if every child wakes up in the morning and knows: *I am a Unique Self. I am evolution in person. I am an Outrageous Lover, and I have unique Outrageous Acts of Love to perform.*

Barbara Marx Hubbard, my evolutionary partner in this church, I miss you so much. Before church today, I was listening to the sermon that you were going to give; we were talking about your sermon. The words kept going through my mind, which you loved so much, *the promise will be kept*. Friends, the promise will be kept. We are the Gospel Church. We are the new Gospel, which is the new story. There's room for everyone, and we desperately need everyone.

We are da Vinci in Florence, at that moment in which premodernity—before the Renaissance—was rocked and shocked in Europe, particularly by the Black Death, which was just too much. The threat and the pain was too much, and there was only one thing to do: to tell a new story, which was the story of modernity. We are da Vinci together. **We are telling a new story: The Universe: A Love Story. It's the emergence of *Homo amor*.**

Amor means love; *its insides are lined with love.* Love is not ordinary love just between human beings—we've exiled love. We've exiled love from the cosmic realm to only the human realm, and in the human realm, only the love of one person—and then only a particular kind of love. Love is actually that which moves the sun and the stars. Love is not mere human sentiment; love is the heart of existence itself, and it awakens in us—*Homo amor.*

IN PRAYER, WE TURN TO THE INFINITE INTIMATE WHO KNOWS OUR NAME

We are about to turn to prayer. One of the things we're doing is we're reclaiming prayer, and that's so important. Immanuel Kant, the philosopher, said, *In modernity, the one thing you're most embarrassed about is to have a friend find you praying* because we lost what prayer was, and the religions distorted prayer. The religions often described prayer as turning to a God who's a cosmic vending machine owned by that religion. You put in a quarter (you put in a prayer), and you get a horse and buggy (you get some goods). That's all wonderful, but that's not what prayer is.

Prayer is not to a god who's a cosmic vending machine. The god we don't believe in doesn't exist. Notice that we're reclaiming words here—that's what we have to do. Sixty-five to seventy percent of the world lives in a religion, and we ignore that—we can't bypass religion.

Religion is the human intuition of the human being to form a life of meaning in relation to ultimate value. It's the ontology, it's the great mystery, ever unfolding of Reality. And that great mystery is intimate. The god you don't believe in doesn't exist; we reclaim God in the deepest highest sense.

In the truest ontology, God is the Infinity of Intimacy.

That's what we're reclaiming, and we're downloading this into the core of Cosmos. God is the Infinity of Intimacy. Imagine your most intimate moment, and then exponentialize that. God is the Infinity of Intimacy who knows my name.

17

We ask a question: *Can you hear me speaking?*

The answer is, *you can hear me speaking.*

I say to you, *How do you hear me speaking?*

Well, maybe it's your ears. But we know it's more than ears; you don't hear just with ears. Ears are an expression of your intelligence and consciousness that hears me.

Then I say to you, *If your consciousness and your intelligence hears Marc speaking, is your consciousness and your intelligence separate from the larger field of intelligence and consciousness?*

The answer is, *Of course not.*

This is called a pointing-out instruction in Tibetan Buddhism. We've borrowed this pointing-out instruction, and we've created this new pointing-out instruction for church that can literally change the fabric and source code of Reality. Here it is. If you hear me with your consciousness and intelligence, and you know—we understand it, it's self-evident—that your consciousness and intelligence is not separate from the larger field of consciousness and intelligence. Could it be that when I speak, when I pray, the larger field of consciousness and intelligence doesn't hear me? Can your intelligence hear me and the larger field can't hear me? Of course not.

That pointing-out instruction, as you got it, you just lived into the enlightenment of what we call *God in the second-person.*

God is the Infinity of Intimacy that knows my name. That's not a dogma of the Church. That's a realization.

I was talking to John Welwood, who was a great guy. He passed away a few weeks ago. He did some of the most important work in the contemporary spiritual scene. He actually coined the term "Wake Up and Grow Up."

We met a few years ago, and John said to me: *Marc, I've heard great things about you. But I heard that you're really off, that you believe in prayer. Like, you believe in prayer, are you serious?*

John was a major Buddhist realized meditator.

I said, *John, what do you believe in?*

John says, *I believe in awareness.*

I said, *John, why do you believe in the dogma of awareness?*

John said, *I don't believe in the* dogma *of awareness. It's not a dogma, it's a realization; I know it.*

I said, *John, prayer is not a dogma, it's a realization.*

In that second, he got it.

I've shared this with my beloved friend, Ken Wilber, and as a result of these conversations, we developed what we call the three faces of God.

We actually begin to realize: I turn to God who's the Infinity of Intimacy, who holds my holy and broken *Hallelujah*. Prayer is not a dogma, it's a realization.

Friends, do you know how lonely it is to live a life without your best friend? The Infinity of Intimacy that yearns for you, that desires you, that wants to love you open in every second, that knows every detail of your holy and your broken *Hallelujah*.

That's our hymn, and we go inside. Friends, what are we doing here? What's our intention? We're playing a larger game. We're participating in the evolution of love.

"Hallelujah,'" Leonard Cohen. [See Appendix]

Oh my god, *I couldn't feel so I tried to touch*. It's the holy and the broken *Hallelujah*.

Prayer affirms the dignity of personal need.

- We're reclaiming prayer for Cosmos.
- We are active agents of Conscious Evolution.
- We are unique intimate expressions and configurations of intimacy.
- We cannot cross this 11th hour alone.
- We are partnering with the Infinity of Intimacy.

We don't begin with saving the world. We are so committed to the politics of love. We are so committed to this being the activist church that actually takes us across the threshold. But we don't bypass our personal need. **We affirm the dignity of personal need and the dignity of our tears and of our longing.**

The word *Hallelujah* means *holelut*: drunken intoxication, and *hallel*: pristine praise. I invite everyone. When I say *I*, I mean *I* as in the Goddess, *I* as in *We* in the Evolutionary Church. We say *I pray for*, and we ask for everything. I want to actually bring down the prayer because we know in neuroscience, when I bring it down in writing, something happens.

I AM AN OUTRAGEOUS LOVER COMMITTING OUTRAGEOUS ACTS OF LOVE

Friends, we're mad lovers. The only way to be sane in the world is to be a mad lover, that's what Rumi says. Rumi says, *I want to be with the rogues and the courtesans and the wild saints*. Let's be mad lovers together. We're Outrageous Lovers.

I want to know what love is, I know you can show me. Friends, Outrageous Acts of Love! Who am I? I'm an Outrageous Lover, and I commit Outrageous Acts of Love. But that's not an aphorism, it's not a metaphor. That's the whole point. It's not a New Age idea. It's actually the nature of Reality, that which drives Reality.

Evolution is the evolution of intimacy. **Intimacy is the Eros, the Outrageous Love, that seeks ever greater contact and ever greater wholeness**. That's core to the codes of the Church, which are based on the best interior and exterior sciences available in the world today.

Oh my god, to actually know that that's my true identity. The best integration of interior and exterior sciences is the realization that Reality *is* the evolution of intimacy. Intimacy is Eros, Outrageous Love, that awakens uniquely in me, as me, and through me. I'm a unique configuration of Outrageous Love. I'm an Outrageous Lover, that's who I am. I'm an Outrageous Lover, and what do Outrageous Lovers do? They commit Outrageous Acts of Love.

As we are here in the One Church to reclaim love as religion, at the beginning of articulating what might be a world religion and a world spirituality, in which all religions have a place, but there's a shared framework. Because we know that *we need a shared framework, a shared Universe Story,* to respond to the global intimacy disorder that's at the core of this moment between utopia and dystopia. In this moment, I'm an Outrageous Lover. We're Outrageous Lovers; we're a band of Outrageous Lovers. I am outrageously loving you, Barbara, as I'm about to turn the word to you. As you would always say, *let's go the whole way in this lifetime.* Evolutionary Church, let's go the whole way in this lifetime. Let's do this together.

Let's now see or listen to a clip of Barbara speaking, recorded when she was still alive.

WE NEED TO INTEGRATE THE LOCAL SELF, ESSENTIAL SELF, AND UNIVERSAL SELF

I (Barbara) am filled with these prayers, and am feeling that when we pray, the love that we have for oneself and for one another is actually reaching all of us simultaneously. I would like to begin this sermon just with a collection of prayers, joining one another. I'm seeing that, in every unique prayer, there's a voice of a chorus that is arising among us to reinforce every prayer by being together as we do it. For this, I give a great deal of thanks.

My sermon today is holding on what Marc has given us as the code:

> To give up being a victim when victimhood is a lie is not true.
> To not take less or more responsibility is the key to the evolution
> of love.

If I take more responsibility, then I have to react. If I take less responsibility, then I can't go within and see what actually needs to be held inside me.

I'd like to share how it is that I do this myself. I have a phrase that has been extremely helpful to me, which is: *to go the whole way in this lifetime*. There's a double entendre in that. One is, of course, to give everything—i.e. your unique expression—the whole way in this lifetime; you leave nothing out that you are here to express.

Whenever I feel victimized, I look within to see, is there more in me in precisely this particular place in which I'm being criticized? Is there something in me that could arise so strongly? Because I've been victimized, I find within myself a strain around that form. For example, loneliness. If I feel loneliness, I'm not going the whole way. Because I need to look inside to see where the oneness is, where the connectivity is, where I'm part of the source of creation and everybody in it. Loneliness is a trigger in myself, and in ourselves, to overcome that pain. Every single place where I may, or you may feel a victim, is actually a space for you to discover your wholeness in so doing.

In my own work, I've had a series of selves that are corresponding pretty close to Marc's in some ways. **In order to go the whole way, I need to integrate all selves of my being**, otherwise there's a space for this victimhood position to come in. In my language, there are three selves that I have been working to integrate. One is a local self, which would be the separate self that doesn't feel connected to anything, but even worse, it tends to be critical of almost everything that happens to me. It's the inner critic, and the inner critic—which is separate—has to be received. This is what I've discovered, it's an egoic self. Instead of being eliminated or killed, the local self is invited to speak, and invited to speak its full story of what it's criticizing and where it feels left out.

Now, the part of me that is hearing the local self say that is what I've called the Essential Self, and I think that's very close to the Unique Self. **The Essential Self is the true essence of my being as I now am**. It's a self that has the soul in it. It has the impulse of creation in it. When that self listens to the separated itself, it can listen to it without being victimized. A big point of not being victimized is to not be *self*-victimized by self-criticism. I would say the greatest victimization that most of us have is being criticized by that part of yourself that is disapproving or left out or distressed. I have had many conversations, and I did this in large classes when I was teaching, where everybody had to hear their own local self and actually speak it out on these large milestone calls, and have the Essential Self or Unique Self— or that part of yourself that is truly who you are uniquely—respond to it.

The Essential Self responds to the separate itself, the egoic self, and it often learns something from it. The ego is not always wrong when it's criticizing or victimizing you, and that may be true when others are victimizing you; there's often some truth to it. But instead of just reacting against that victimization, you are able to actually learn from it and hear it out. If somebody is actually victimizing me, and I hear it out because I've learned to handle my own inner critic, it's often quite destabilizing to the person who's victimizing you. It's not easy to do, because there's something in the victimizer that is actually afflicting them to attack you. If you are bold enough to be able to feel that and have them feel it, you have really done a major job in handling it. So that's the thing, the local self is brought in through the Essential Self.

Now in my own vocabulary, the Essential Self is also now activated by what I have called the Universal Self. That is part of Marc's own, I would say, Evolutionary Unique Self.

> *The Universal Self has a memory of the future self; the Universal Self knows what you are becoming. It knows the potential in you that has not yet been fulfilled.*

On the one hand, you have the critical self, then you have the current Unique Self, and then you have the self that can blossom out the whole way. This is when we give our gifts the whole way; not only our prayers, but our gifts. I'm giving my gift the whole way by my vocational arousal, no matter how far out it might possibly seem. In my case, it's very similar to what Marc is saying, and what we're saying as a church—it's a planetary awakening in love.

If you think of this for a moment, **your Universal Self is coded with who you are becoming and with your greatest mission on Earth**. It is actually coded with your unique mission. But it's usually so grand, so big, and so great that you have to *not* allow it in. Just like you don't allow the ego in, you don't allow the universal or the greatness of yourself in. When you are able to allow that in, what happens for me is then there's a whole self. The whole self is able to give up being a victim, give up being a victimizer, and is able to evolve itself in love.

UNGUARD OUR HEARTS AND LOVE MAD

Oh my god, Barbara, you're going to hold the sermon space today—I'm just going to say something very briefly. I want to just say something for realsies. In Hebrew, the word for money is *kessef*: yearning. What I really yearn for, where I actually make a contribution, where I actually count out my funds, that's my real set of values.

So, if I'm listening but I can't quite get there, there's a very beautiful text that says that your true language is either the language you make love in, or the language you count money in. That's a mystical text. We are love in action. We are *amor* in action. I really want to invite everyone to put this in practice. A whole bunch of people have already done this, and I—as well as we, the church, and the evolution of love itself—could not be more appreciative.

This is our church. It's not my church. It's not Barbara's church. It's the Goddess's church. We are love in action. Evolution is awake through us, and evolution is love in action. We are love in action, and the action right now is to step in. This is really important. *The promise will be kept*, but the promise can't be kept unless we step in and we make this move together.

Let's just do two more steps. When we give up victimhood, we can actually let our armor go. Because we're armored; our hearts are guarded. Evolution is love in action, we are love in action, and the action here is to give up victimhood. **When we give up victimhood, we remove our armor; we unguard our hearts.** Who's willing to be here with me? Can we be now with unguarded hearts?

- We get to be excited.
- We can love madly.
- We are Outrageous Lovers.
- We're writing each other Outrageous Love Letters.
- We unguard our hearts.
- We move from Homo armor to *Homo amor*, and we confess our greatness.

Here's what I want to invite everyone to say. It's a long sentence, it's Barbara's sentence, and I love this sentence:

I'm going to go the whole way in this lifetime.

Who's up for that? That's my commitment. How deep is your love, right? I'm going the whole way in this lifetime. We're not doing it by ourselves. We're doing it together. We love each other, and we love madly. **Because**

loving mad is the only way to be sane. I'm going to go the whole way in this lifetime.

The One Church, in which we are saying not the religion of love, but love as religion—One Church reclaiming love as religion towards a politics of love.

One Church is going to go the whole way in this lifetime, as a band of Outrageous Lovers, as da Vinci, as the Gospel Church in the civil rights movement.

CHAPTER THREE

OUR MORAL COMMUNITY
IS ALL OF REALITY

Episode 143 — July 6, 2019

WE'RE TAKING RESPONSIBILITY TO BE THE EVOLUTION OF LOVE

We're sitting in this place, and we set our intention in this moment. Our beautiful and holy intention is to actually be what we call *love in action*. We set our intention to be the unique expression of the evolutionary impulse, moving in each of us individually at this moment between utopia and dystopia. We intend to commit our Outrageous Acts of Love, to engage in our deepest transformation, and be a voice like the Gospel Church was in the Civil Rights movement, like a new church always needs to be. Like it was in Bethlehem, as Paul was on the road to Damascus and experienced the resurrected Christ and was blinded for three days, and then spent the rest of his life speaking the new Gospel.

We are a Gospel Church—we're bringing the Good News, and the Good News is the new story. It's the new Universe Story, the new story of identity. The new story which answers the great question of *who are you*? We are delighted, and we are urgent. But we are urgent not in an

27

egoic sense, we're ecstatically urgent. We're ecstatically urgent because we know that, literally, we're on the brink today.

I don't know if everyone knows that in Madras, India, which actually probably has about 40 million people in it, *there's no water.*

The only water that's in Madras is being brought in on trucks, and there's enormous suffering. That's a signal of potential things to come—unless we reconfigure the essential source code structures of our world.

So we are that voice.

We are that voice that's actually standing at the brink, at the leading edge, with radical humility, and saying: *This is our responsibility.* It's a new lineage, and the lineage is: *we're taking responsibility to transform ourselves and to transform literally the source code itself—to be the evolution of love.*

I could not be more delighted, more ecstatic, and more honored to be with every single person in this Evolutionary Church. Ten thousand people have registered all over the world, and we're just beginning to grow a grassroots movement. There should be many more in all corners of the world, people starting Evolutionary Churches—churches of one love and one heart. Oh my god, we have to rip our hearts open again and again.

AMOR: THE UNIVERSE FEELS, AND THE UNIVERSE FEELS LOVE

We're about to go into *amor*. The church of *Homo amor*, the church of Evolutionary Love. When we say love, we don't mean just romantic love. We love romantic love, but romantic love is an expression of the core love that animates the Cosmos itself.

My lineage master Solomon, who was the great holder of Goddess energy, who married a thousand wives—the lineage says it's because he was holding the energy of Goddess. Maybe each wife married a thousand Solomons.

This energy of Goddess, the energy of She, is the realization that *its insides are lined with love*.

- It's the energy of God/Goddess.
- It's the energy of ontology.
- It's the energy of divinity.
- It's the realization, again—that *its insides are lined with love*, meaning not ordinary love, but Outrageous Love.

Outrageous Love is the love that moves the sun and other stars. Outrageous Love is not a mere human sentiment; we've exiled love to its mere human sentiment. Outrageous Love is the heart of existence itself. In Evolutionary Church, we are all about one thing: awakening as Outrageous Lovers. Every single one of us, fully awake, loving our way to enlightenment, Homo armor to *Homo amor* and then committing our Outrageous Acts of Love that Reality demands from us, needs from us, and yearns for from us, as the centerpiece of our life.

That's the whole church, activating a Unique Self Symphony all over the world—human beings awakening to our true identity as unique incarnations of intimacy and Outrageous Love, and then spontaneously generating the next phase of evolution, awakening as evolution conscious in us, as unique beloveds committing Outrageous Acts of Love.

Here's the essence of *amor*. **Interiors are real. The Universe feels, and the Universe feels love.** I remember when I shared this the first time with Barbara, she must have called me and sent me maybe 15–20 emails a day for two weeks because she knew how to be ecstatic.

Evolution is the evolution of intimacy. We live in an Intimate Universe.

WE PARTICIPATE IN THE THREE FACES OF GOD

This is our *dharma*. We say these words every week. God is not the ethnocentric, homophobic, premodern, responsible for so many cruelties god, with whom you put in a prayer and you get out a car. No, that's not the god we're talking about. The god you don't believe in doesn't exist.

We participate with God. God holds us, God is beyond us, and God lives in us, as us, and through us. We're creating a participatory spirituality, where we are held by the Divine and the Divine holds us. The Divine, at His/Her/Its core, is the Infinity of Power.

The power that moves through and animates exponentially all of Cosmos, and hundreds of billions of galaxies and hundreds of billions of light years, and universes and multiverses beyond imagination, all of that is the infinite power of divinity.

Yet, Divinity lives not only in third-person, that infinite energetic movement of dazzling complexity beyond imagination. God lives in second-person. God holds me. God knows me. Yes, God is inside of me, that's first-person. God lives in me, as me, and through me, and uniquely expresses in a particular configuration of intimacy, which is God configuring as me and transfiguring me. That's God in first-person.

PRAYER AFFIRMS THE DIGNITY OF PERSONAL NEED

But in prayer, we turn to God in second-person. We turn to God who holds us and knows our name. We turn to the God who's the Mother, God who's the Father, God who's the Beloved and the Lover. God who is not merely intimacy. As we say in the church of Evolutionary Love, God is the Infinity of Intimacy that knows my name, that is with me in every moment. We may live lives sometimes of quiet desperation, as Thoreau wrote back in *Walden Pond*. But here's the promise, and the promise will be kept: *we never live lives of* lonely *desperation, because we're never alone.* It never happens. **Goddess, She, is always with us, holding us literally in our holy and our broken *Hallelujah.***

Here's the meditation that we do every week, let's shut our eyes for a second. Imagine the infinite force of Cosmos, God in the third-person, moving through every law of physics and every law of mathematics, which makes a supernova look like a vague swat of a fly. The supernova barely exists in relation to what it participates in. The supernova participates in the supernova of the Infinity of Divine Power—God in the third person.

All of that, now sitting in a chair next to you, looking at you, yearning for you, wanting to receive your holy and broken *Hallelujah*, wanting to know everything, loving you open, and holding you, more infinitely tender, with more alive desire than you've ever experienced in your life exponentially squared. That's God in the second person.

That's a true realization. I'm blessed to hold that realization, you're blessed. Let's hold it together. I'm going to give it to you so it's your realization. You can feel it and know it in this second. That holy and broken *Hallelujah*—everything—She's holding it all.

Homo amor turns to the Infinity of Intimacy and prays. Maybe you've never prayed, and maybe you pray every day. But prayer means that I actually bring it down and actually speak it. Prayer is always, we say, *b'peh*. I enunciate it, I speak it, I say it, and I articulate my personal need. My personal need is holy.

Prayer affirms the dignity of personal need.

I ask first for myself and for my uncle and my friend and my brother. I affirm the radical, gorgeous, infinite dignity of my life, and then I move beyond my life. I move to my friends (egocentric), to my people and community, and to the world (worldcentric), and then for Reality itself.

Let's pray in a different way. Let's pray to know what love is. *I want to know what love is.* It's not ordinary love. We're moving from victims to players. We're expressions of Outrageous Love. We are the church that's the politics of Evolutionary Love. We want to change the source code itself. *I want to know what love is*, let's pray together. Let's feel that prayer just blowing us away. Let's do the words. Let's sing it, and let's dance it.

31

Oh my god, *I want to know what love is, I want you to show me.* "I Want to Know What Love Is," Foreigner [See Appendix].

MY MORAL COMMUNITY INCLUDES ALL OF REALITY

Evolutionary Love Code:

> Reality is driven by pleasure.
>
> The highest pleasure is the pleasure of transformation.
>
> Transformation equals evolution.
>
> The highest pleasure of transformation is to know that your transformation transforms everything.
>
> The highest transformation possible is to participate in the transformation of God.
>
> The highest pleasure of evolution is to know that your evolution evolves everything, and the highest evolution possible is to participate in the evolution of God.

Reality is motivated by pleasure. We live in a world of outrageous pain, and Barbara is going to talk about the pain a little bit in a sermon today as well—and about the joy; the pain in Madras today. It's one world. It's one love. It's one heart.

Here's the sentence.

The single most important thing we can do in the world today is for people to realize that your moral community is all of Reality.

My moral community is not only my son and daughter and husband; my son and daughter and my husband are beautiful. Or living by myself, connected with this friend and that friend—that's beautiful. That's egocentric moral community, that's beautiful. Then there's my wider people—that's an ethnocentric moral community, and that's also gorgeous.

But actually, my moral community is every human being on the planet. If people are thirsty in Madras, then I'm thirsty. My moral community is the planet itself—and not just the planet, but Reality itself. Because we're in a moment when Reality is about to intertexture. **We're standing before a phase shift in history, which is as great as the phase shift from single cellular to multicellular life.** It's exploding, but there's no source code.

We need a source code—it's the most desperate need of our generation. We need to take all of the world's great traditions in every period (premodern, modern, and postmodern), Hinduism, etc. We're going to have with us next week, my dear beloved friend and colleague, Sally Kempton, who's really one of the great holders of the Hindu lineage, who's going to be doing a five-minute beautiful meditation on the code.

We need this code. This code basically is bringing together all of the great premodern traditions, all of the great modern wisdom streams, with all the insights of postmodernity that were important. My friend Jordan Peterson didn't understand postmodernity. He went back to modernity, which is important; he understood modernity well. But postmodernity has important things to say. We weave them all together, and then together we articulate the Goddess speaking in this moment. It's the unmediated expression of the best story, rooted not in dogma but in *dharma*—the best integrations of all the premodern, modern, and postmodern wisdom streams, and all of their validated insights.

Here we go. This is how we begin to know my moral community is the whole thing.

The first thing is, I have to know what Reality is. Reality is motivated by pleasure. Actually, the interior of Reality is pleasure. I call that sometimes quantum hedonism, and **quantum hedonism means that at the molecular level, allurement holds the whole thing**. The same allurement that brought us all to church today—the same allurement that moves us to create, that

33

moves us to look at a sunset, that in fact moves us towards everything—all of our life is guided by that allurement.

I was sitting not that long ago with Werner Erhard, who started the entire movement of EST and Landmark. Werner said to me, *if you want to give me one idea that I don't have, that I can actually bring in and change everything, what would it be?*

I said, *allurement*. I said, *Werner, we're here talking to each other because we were allured*. Werner just got so excited. He said, oh my God, *I didn't have that distinction*. That's what he called an *on the court distinction*. He said, *I promise you, I'm going to spend the rest of my life working with that distinction.*

"Reality is motivated by pleasure" means that Reality on the Inside of the Inside is allurement; gravity and electromagnetic attraction are expressions of allurement. Now, what does allurement want to do? Allurement wants transformation. **The movement of evolution is towards transformation.** When nature—Reality, the self-organizing Universe, the Infinity of Intimacy—brings separate parts together to form larger wholes, that motivation is allurement, and that larger whole is a transformation. The parts get transformed; they're deeper, they're more whole, they're more alive, they have more capacity. They've recognized new possibility, because divinity is the Possibility of Possibility.

THERE ARE SIX LEVELS OF PLEASURE

Reality is motivated by pleasure. There's a hedonism; there's a pleasure all the way up and all the way down. But it's to know my pleasure. My pleasure is ice cream at level one. But at level two, my pleasure might be love in relationships. At level three, my pleasure might be meaning-making and standing for a noble cause. At level four, my pleasure might be knowing my True Self enlightenment, loving my way to enlightenment. At level five, my pleasure might be living my Unique Self. Then at the highest, level six, my pleasure is knowing my transformation.

I just went through six levels of pleasure.

1. Level one: all the physical senses. All the natural and beautiful senses of the world, that's level one pleasure. It's got a counterfeit form, and it's got a sacred and authentic form.

2. Level two: love and affection in relationships. All of level one can't get you any of level two.

3. Level three: standing for a cause. Standing deep, structurally, excitedly, passionately, fully, with massive commitment, being productive for a cause, that's level three. All of level two, love and affection in relationships, can't get you any of level three.

4. Level four: knowing your true nature, the pleasure of wisdom, of knowing, of gnosis. All of level three can't get you any of level four.

5. Level five: your radical Unique Self creativity. It doesn't always mean what you love doing. It's what you can do in the circle of intimacy and influence that's most needed by Reality. Sometimes that meets your delight, and sometimes it doesn't. But it's your unique gift at a particular moment in time. My Unique Self creativity as a response to divinity that needs my service, that's the fifth level of pleasure.

6. But the sixth level, which is the subject of this code, is the highest pleasure: transformation.

Reality is motivated by pleasure, and the highest pleasure is transformation. Transformation and evolution are the same, they mean the same thing. Then the highest pleasure of transformation is to know that your transformation transforms everything.

You get how shocking that is?

- If I own the shadow, and I transform myself;
- If I forgive, if I open my heart in a way that it has never been open;
- If I take my part of responsibility in a contribution system;
- If I'm fearless in actually opening my heart when my heart

feels closed.

It's easy to open my heart when I'm just outraged with desire and Outrageous Love, when I'm all in. That's easy. It's when my heart wants to close.

And there's a thousand reasons that we move to close our hearts.

- There's all sorts of agendas of power.
- There's agendas of shame.
- There's agendas of fear.
- There's agendas of anger.

But to be *Homo amor*, to be Outrageous Love, is to open my heart again and again. Not just to love the moment open—I love the moment open by loving my heart open—but actually **when my heart feels most like wanting to close, when I feel most like wanting to contract, I blow my heart open and I transform**.

That transformation that takes place on the Inside of the Inside of my heart—one love, one heart—that transformation transforms everything beyond imagination.

I'm going to turn the word to Barbara. Barbara, it's been such a delight to be with you in Evolutionary Church, and it's such a delight to be with you today.

The Evolutionary Church now is the place in the world in which you're doing *dharma* and you're giving *dharma*. It's so gorgeous to be together. I write Barbara on WhatsApp, because that's one of the places where we talked to each other; we talk a lot. Barbara, this is one of your favorite codes, I'm so delighted.

THE PLEASURE OF TRANSFORMATION: PARTNERS IN THE EVOLUTIONARY PROCESS

Thank you for the pleasure of transformation that we're in together here. As we are praying and as you are speaking, the first thing I celebrate is the new story of creation. This church, as far as I know, is the church that has accessed the nature of the new story of creation. The discovery that from the origin, from the Big Bang all the way through for billions and billions of years—as we've learned through Teilhard de Chardin, as we've learned through Sri Aurobindo, as we've learned through Marc Gafni, as we've learned through Barbara Hubbard, and all the rest of us—**we are an expression of a multi-billion-year yearning of Divine creativity**. For what?

If I were God, what would I be yearning for? I'd be yearning, first of all, for an Evolutionary Church; a church in which there's my yearning for people to recognize they are expressions of God, and that they are co-creators with God.

And they are co-creators with God at a time when the God force on this planet is jumping to a new order—of complexity, of creativity, of power, of danger, of genius, of potential—that has never been seen before on planet Earth.

I'm setting the scene for us—not only to see the billions of years that came before us, but the exact moment we're in. It's hard to imagine a shift from single cell to multicell. It's hard to really imagine what evolution did to get from a multicellular creature into a coherent animal. Those jumps are awesome. Then the jump from the animal to the most intelligent pre-human. I've seen these pictures of *Homo erectus, Homo habilis, Homo Neanderthal*, doing amazing things from just the animal world.

Then comes in this unknown quantity called *Homo sapiens*, who looked pretty much the same. But what was God doing as *Homo sapiens*? **Homo sapiens came into the scene of these billions of years of tremendous efforts, five mass extinctions, and billions of species going extinct**. The pain of it has to be realized within the glory of it, otherwise it's too painful. Much destruction to create so much of the newness! Well, that's what happened.

This is the precise moment of recognition that Reality is designed for pleasure, when we are also feeling both the possibility of a de-evolutionary sequence on planet Earth that could lead to the loss of our life support system. The is same power of the impulse in every one of us going towards fulfillment of our potential, at a time of a quantum shift, or a jump, or newness, that has never been seen before on earth. We are holding this together.

When I think of the early days of Christianity, Jesus was like a new person.

- If you've seen me, you've seen the Father.
- You will do the work that I do, and even greater works will you do in the fullness of time.

Okay, Jesus, this must be exactly the fullness of time that you were speaking of.

Now, let's then look at our code: Reality is designed for pleasure. Reality is the realization of potential. The whole idea of allurement and intimacy and contact has given us the pattern that **God creates more newness by joining separate parts to make a new whole**. That had to be a pleasure, or we just couldn't possibly have done it.

So, while we're looking at the story of evolution with all the pain, we have to feel internally all the pleasure. Not just our own, but the quarks with the quarks, atoms with atoms, and so on and so forth. Love at the core of the evolutionary process now becoming our allurement, our realization, and our contact and intimacy with Source, with the process of creation, with each other—not only with our own personal potential, but the potential of the whole system.

God made it so that the highest pleasure is transformation. Now, why is this? When you think of all the suffering, all the pain, all the agony of change, and people getting lost and getting hurt and killed—at the same time, transformation is pleasurable when I am identifying with the predicament of God. If I were God wanting to be sure that humans could become godlike, that we could become co-creators with the Creator, I could not have done this as a robotic universe. I had to do this by us feeling the pain, so that we could become aware of the impulse of creation.

We are entering into this radical period of change. When we align with It, the big *It*. It animates us with pleasure. It animating you and me with Its pleasure, God's pleasure, in being able to give to the human beings, not only the answer to our needs and our prayers, but the answer to our yearning for greatness, for potentiality, for fulfillment of divine potential.

---

*Evolution is incarnating and
embodying itself as us.*

Then this beautiful phrase: the highest pleasure of transformation is the knowing that your transformation transforms everything. Why would that be so? If the intention of creation is to create beings ever more able to co-create with the Divine, and we are at the threshold of transforming everything on this planet—very much as we did from single cell, to multicell, to animal, to human, to evolutionary human, to *Homo universalis* human, able to have the powers we used to attribute to our gods—then **the highest pleasure of transformation is knowing that when we say yes to the potential within us, connected to the potential within others, animated by the potential of God, it's ecstatic!**

I want to offer here that when we source this source code of evolution— which is the impulse of creation, sourcing evolution for billions of years— we're doing what is the greatest impulse of our destiny: changing the source code of culture. How do we really do that? Yes, we write the books about it, but how do we write the books about it unless we are It? Unless we are Source sourcing, Source creating, Source evolving?

I'll say in conclusion that this is the ultimate ecstasy of universal evolution— that we're feeling ecstasy of evolution, the joy of wholeness. The passion of

God's purpose being our purpose—fulfilling all of us toward an awakening of the new human and the new humanity, in a universe undoubtedly filled with other intelligences—being born right now as a new species. Thank you, God—I am Source, sourcing itself.

Marc, I turn to you in asking for our contribution together. Our contribution to the Evolutionary Church is the contribution to the evolution of humanity, because there's no place else I know of on Earth where it's being codified and expressed and made real. I don't know of any other, it's awesomely precious.

Even the word "contribution"—I think it would be good for us to realize the ecstasy of creativity and our potentials through participating with each other; this is our contribution to the process of creation. Our financial contribution to this is going to make it possible for this to deepen on a world scale. I believe we have a mission as great as the mission of St. Paul on the road to Damascus, where he had an experience of the resurrected Christ and went blind for three days—and then he changed the world.

WE ARE ALL THE HIGH PRIESTS AND PRIESTESSES

We're the One World Church. We're the church of Evolutionary Love. We're reclaiming love as religion, but we're reclaiming the evolution of love towards a pragmatic politics of love. Let's contribute, because contribution is so essential. If you're thinking that Barbara is our High Priestess, or Marc is our High Priest, there are no High Priests and High Priestesses here.

I'm going to cite you a verse from one of the original great spiritual texts: *Ve'at'em ti'hyu mam'lekh'et kohanim ve'goy kadosh*—you shall be before me a kingdom of priests.[1]

Here in Evolutionary Church, we are a kingdom of High Priests and High Priestesses. Yes, there's *dharma*. Yes, there's transmission. Yes, there's teaching. But ultimately, the next Buddha is a Buddha and a *sangha*.

---

1 Book of Exodus, 19:6.

The *sangha* itself, the band of Outrageous Lovers itself, you committing your Outrageous Acts of Love, us coming together as the self-organizing Universe in person, enacting the next stage and the next great turning of the source code, which is the emergence of *Homo amor*. Each of us participates in that emergence in this Unique Self Symphony, and we're moving in Evolutionary Church towards a planetary awakening in love through Unique Self Symphonies.

Let me say that again. The stated absolute intention of the church is: a planetary awakening in Outrageous Love through Unique Self Symphonies. When we all come together and we actually live that Unique Self and give that unique gift, we look in each other's eyes and we say: *How could anyone ever tell you that you are anything less than beautiful? How could anyone ever tell you that you are less than whole? How could anyone fail to notice here in* Evolutionary Church, the One World Church of Evolutionary Love, *that our love is a miracle that Cosmos needs?* That's not arrogance, it's holy audacity.

- We're going to speak the story.
- We're going to take responsibility.
- We're going to participate in the evolution of love.
- We're going to stand at the brink.

Are we excited? We are excited!

Are we evangelical in the sense of bringing the Good News? We are!

Are we filled sometimes with pain? Of course we are.

But ultimately, we love our hearts open. **We speak into the pain with activism**, with radical personal love, and we literally love it open for the sake of evolving the source code. This is us, we're the High Priests and the High Priestesses.

CHAPTER FOUR

GOD LOOKS AT US WITH A GOOD EYE; I SEE YOU AND I STAND FOR YOU

Episode 144 — July 13, 2019

SEEING EACH OTHER WITH AYIN TOVAH, A GOOD EYE

We're going to do this beautiful and gorgeous code today, which is about intimacy. I just want to say one thing about intimacy. There's a very beautiful word; I was just thinking about it a minute ago. For whatever reason, in the last couple of weeks, I've just had tears in my eyes all the time. A friend of mine said to me, *I only trust a person who always has tears in their eyes.* Tears are the beautiful expression of being connected—our hearts open, we can feel.

There's lots of kinds of tears. I had the great privilege of writing a book on tears many years ago that we're actually just going to publish, I hope this year, about 12 kinds of tears. We actually know now biochemically that different kinds of tears have different constitutions. Isn't that wild? **Tears mean you're connected to the inside.**

In these last couple of weeks, I've been thinking about this beautiful phrase called *Ayin tovah*, which means a *good*

eye. Ayin ra'ah is a bad eye, and that's where the English idea of the Evil Eye came from. But it's not about an Evil Eye in a kind of weird, magic way. It's much more mystical and much more beautiful. ***Ayin tovah* is a good eye, it means *I see with the eyes of love.***

- I see you.
- I hold you in all of your beauty, and all of your imperfection, and all of your mistakes, and all of your greatness.
- I can hold and be excited about your greatness.
- I can be excited about your transformation.
- I can be excited and hold your imperfection.
- I can hold your broken *Hallelujah* and your holy *Hallelujah*.
- I can hold it all because I have an *ayin tovah*: a good eye.

God looks at us with a good eye. God yearns to be intimate with us. God holds our holy and our broken *Hallelujah*. **To be an Outrageous Lover is to say, *I see you*.** Sometimes when someone listens to us talk, and we feel they're not looking at us with a good eye, we sort of stumble; we try too hard. Because we don't feel the intimacy of being seen with a good eye. To be an Outrageous Lover means that—not just in the good times, not just in the ecstatic times, but in the hardest times—we see each other with a good eye; we hold each other. We move to just be madly in love with each other in the most complex times. That's what it means.

Can we actually get close? Can we get closer than close? Can we take that sense of having no distance between us and see each other with a good eye? That's the evolutionary move; that's the evolutionary impulse. Usually, the only people we see with a good eye are: my son, my daughter, my husband, if that, in a functional family. But that's very narrow. **We can actually expand and see more and more people with a good eye, and bring more and more people into our heart.**

At church, we see each other with a good eye. We're intimate. We feel each other. Then we come together as a church, and we create this new configuration of intimacy. When we say church, we mean synagogue and mosque and zendo; we are the One-World Church. We are the church that's reclaiming love as religion. We're the church that's actually standing for moving towards a pragmatic politics of love. That's who we are.

We are One-World Church. We're reclaiming love as religion. We're telling the new Universe Story because we know that there's nothing more desperately important today in the world, literally, to alleviate suffering. Because we're about to go through a phase shift in the world, which literally—no exaggeration, no hyperbole—is as dramatic as the move from single-celled to multi-celled life. The entire story is changing.

At this moment, what we need more desperately than anything else is not artificial intelligence, which is algorithmic computational power. We need what we call not AI but AO, which is what I've been working on for the last three months. It's anthro-ontology. Anthro-ontology means: *Anthro*—the human being; and ontology—for real. *The mysteries are within us; love is within us.*

Love is a perception where we can see each other, and we see each other with God's eyes.

We want to create a community of people seeing each other with God's eyes, and then we begin to see the world with God's eyes. But not just in a naïve way. We become activists. We're actually standing for each other's transformation.

To love someone means:

- I stand for your transformation.
- I hold you in your imperfection.
- I hold you in your beauty.
- I'm willing to put myself aside and be in devotion to your greatness, and then let you go all the way in this lifetime.

One of the things I loved about Barbara is she would always say to me, *Marc, I'm standing for you to go the whole way in this lifetime. Marc, will you stand for me to go the whole way in this lifetime*? Barbara and I would work in the Holy of Holies on all the places that we were imperfect, and all the places we made mistakes, because we all make mistakes. We're all imperfect. **The perfect teacher, the perfect philosopher, the perfect anybody doesn't exist**. We're all imperfect vessels for the light. We need to actually fearlessly love each other and fearlessly stand for each other. We're looking at each other with a good eye.

REALITY IS *AMOR*: ITS INSIDES ARE LINED WITH LOVE

We're about to do *amor*, which is our chant. I just want to say a word just to set up the chant: *amor*. *Amor* means love; *amor* means connection. Intimacy means we're connected—we've made contact.

Before church, I just had this long talk with Harville Hendrix.[2] He is a dear and beautiful man. We were very close friends a number of years ago, and we've reconnected. I was sharing with him the *dharma* of church and he was so excited and so delighted, and he said something really beautiful. He talks in terms of interconnectivity. I said to him, *The inside of interconnectivity is intimacy*, and he got it really beautifully. He said: *When you lose interconnectivity, as you're pointing to, the interior is really intimacy—there's actually a rupture in being.*

What happens in relationships is, we're close, then we get farther, but we never look away. It's okay in our relationships to have hard moments. But when we don't look away—even if we go where we go, and we all have different paths to follow in life—but I'm so proud when we don't look away in conflict. Harville said his teacher was Paul Tillich. Paul was one the

---

2   Harville Hendrix is an American author, therapist, and educator best known for developing Imago Relationship Therapy (IRT), a form of couples therapy that aims to help partners heal childhood wounds and deepen emotional connection through conscious communication.

great theologians of our time. Paul said to him, *When there's a rupture in connection, there's a rupture in being itself.*

I just wanted to share that with you.

There's a rupture in being because being is *amor.* That's Solomon; *its insides are lined with love.*

We can come close, we can be super-close, we can be at no distance, we can step back, but we never look away. It's so beautiful. If we can create a world like that—that world of *amor* where we know *its insides are lined with love*—and we can speak it precisely with the memetic codes of the new story—with the new narrative of identity, a new narrative of power, a new narrative of relationship, a new narrative of community, and a new Universe Story—we're literally evolving the memetic source codes of the structure of Cosmos itself. That's *amor*; that's what we mean when we say *amor.*

WE COME TO GOD WITH OUR HOLY AND BROKEN *HALLELUJAH*

We're entering prayer, everyone. In prayer, we ask for everything. In prayer, we begin to feel and resonate the code. The code is about the Infinity of Intimacy. We turn to God not only as the Infinity of Power, but we turn to God as the Infinity of Intimacy. And we say: *God, know me. God, I want to know you. Know my holy and my broken Hallelujah.*

Hallelujah, do you remember this word? *Hallelujah* means, *hallel*: pristine praise, and *holelut*: the brokenness, the drunken intoxication, the fall. **We come to God with our holy and our broken *Hallelujah.*** There's no person on this call, no exceptions, who doesn't have an experience of their holiness and their brokenness. But when we embrace both our holiness and our brokenness, and then we work and we move together, and we know that there's nothing more whole than a broken heart, we come before the Divine and we say: *Take all of me. Hold all of me. Know all of me.*

47

We can bring it all. Rumi says: *I rest it all at your altar, Beloved*. Everything, all of the tears, and all of the laughter, and all of the empty nights, and all of the broken moments, and all of the most pristinely gorgeous right moments in which we confess our greatness and our radiance and our splendor beyond imagination. The holy and the broken *Hallelujah*, we bring it before God.

Not just God who lives in us; God in the first-person. Not just God who is the flowing force of the self-organizing Universe; God in the third-person. But God in the second-person: God who knows my name, who holds me in every moment. The Infinite Personhood of Cosmos in which my personhood participates. We turn to you, God, with our holy and our broken *Hallelujah*.

"Hallelujah,'" Leonard Cohen [See Appendix].

We pray, and we ask for everything. Prayer affirms the dignity of personal need. Prayer affirms the dignity of our holy and broken *Hallelujah*. We ask from our brokenness, and we ask from our wholeness.

We know that God/Goddess, the Infinity of Intimacy, sees us with a good eye.

I ask for everything—personally and collectively—and I ask for my deepest heart's desire, which Barbara is going to talk to us about today.

BREATHING MEDITATION WITH SALLY KEMPTON

Such a joy to be with all of you, and to be with Marc, who is one of the great teachers of love, intimacy, and wisdom that I know. Please, let yourself find a posture where you're comfortable, upright, and aware of the breath. Feel the weight of your sit bones on your seat, feel that you're supported by the earth.

Then with the inhalation, breath in down to the base of the posture. Then with the exhalation, feel the torso lifting up through the crown. Let your awareness come into the heart. You can put your right hand palm down over your heart and your left hand on top of it.

Now with your eyes closed, your upper eyelid resting gently on the lower eyelid, begin to inhale with the feeling that this Intimate Universe is breathing you. **With every breath you draw in, the love at the heart of the universe flows into your heart.** Breathe with the feeling that with every exhalation, that profound, tender, subtle affection—which is the true breath of this world—flows from you and mingles with the particles of love energy that are flowing between us all.

It's very simple. Inhaling with the sense that your inhale of tenderness and affection, that your breath caresses the heart, opening contractions, filling your heart with softness. Then with the exhalation, you offer that breath back into the universe. So it is!

INTIMACY IS SHARED IDENTITY IN THE CONTEXT OF OTHERNESS

From that place of meditation, that place of deep on the Inside of the Inside, God is the Infinity of Intimacy who reveals that the infinite is intimate, not indifferent. We think there are billions of years of empty space. We think there's this vast universe, which is empty, and we wonder how we can find our significance in it.

One of the keys to the *dharma* is that space is not empty; space is actually dancing and dazzled with allurement. **All of the subatomic particles, and all of the atoms, and all of the molecules, are all allured to each other.** Because actually, the infinite which desires intimacy manifests this Intimate Universe, which is this dazzling field of allurement, and then that allurement awakens in us. God is the Infinity of Intimacy, and then the intimacy of Infinity lives all over the universe.

When we look at each other with a good eye, when we hold each other in our holy and our broken *Hallelujah*, then we can actually create a shared identity with each other. Intimacy is shared identity, in the context of otherness; we remain other. **We're always other to each other—as Buber said, *I* and *Thou*—and yet we have a genuine shared identity**.

We have this very limited shared identity. We marry one person, and we say that's the person we have shared identity with—Mr. And Mrs. Smith. That's most beautiful when it works, but also a very narrow form of shared identity. It means you've left out the rest of the world, and you have shared identity with one person; your dog, your son, your daughter, your husband, your wife, maybe your mother, or maybe an uncle.

No, that's a limited shared identity. One of the principles of the church is that we actually want to join genius with each other; we want to be whole mates. Not just role mates where we're raising a family together, not just soul mates where we're looking deeply in each other's eyes and healing each other's wounds, which is beautiful and we can be soul mates with many people. But we want to be whole mates: we want to be looking at a shared horizon, by joining genius, with an actual sense of shared identity. We want the pleasure of genius-joining, the pleasure of that intimacy, the pleasure of creating shared identity for the sake of the evolution of love—creating shared identity for the sake of creating the next step. We want to know that we are addressed personally by the Cosmos.

IN EVERY MOMENT INFINITY WHISPERS TO US AND WE REPLY 'YES'

Evolutionary Love Code:

> God is the Infinity of Intimacy, who reveals that the infinite is intimate and not indifferent. To know God is to know the Intimacy of Infinity, which is to realize that we are personally addressed by the Cosmos in every second. In every second, Infinity asks us an intimate question, whose whisper we can barely hear. While we are often uncertain as to what the question is, we are always certain as to the answer. The answer is always

Yes. Intimacy is unique. Intimacy erases difference and expresses uniqueness.

That's the code. In every second, Infinity asks us an intimate question, whose whisper we can barely hear, and we're often uncertain as to exactly what the question is. But the answer is always Yes. Let's take that deeper. Let's actually see if we can find and listen to the question. **The question always is, what is your deepest heart's desire?** Because your deepest heart's desire is God's desire. Your deepest heart's desire is not your favorite thing to do; that might not be it.

Your deepest heart's desire is to give the most gorgeous and stunning part of myself in devotion, in a way in which I'm fully alive and delighted, which is an expression of Reality having a *me* experience that's unique. **My heart's desire is unique, and my heart's desire is part of the Field of Desire.** My heart's desire expresses itself emotionally, existentially, and physically. It expresses itself in giving my unique gift, and my unique gift is not always public. It's the way I give my unique presence, my unique beingness, and my unique quality of intimacy that Reality desperately needs.

So, Reality turns to me and Reality, the Infinity of Intimacy, says:

- I need you.
- I need your partnership.
- I need to be together with you.
- I want to be together with you.
- I want to join with you.

The Infinity of Intimacy turns to every single one of us and says: Go inside, find the secret chord. That's the secret chord.

My heart's desire is unique. It's part of the Field of Desire, but it is a unique configuration of desire. The Infinity of Intimacy turns to me and you and says, *partner with Me.* Then you ask, well, *How should I partner? What should I do?* The Infinity of Intimacy says, *find your* deepest heart's desire, *and that* deepest heart's desire—this is what Barbara and I talked about all the time—*is the blueprint of our partnership. That's when we become intimate*. **Sometimes our deepest heart's desire is this big public thing, and sometimes it's very intimate, and sometimes it's both**. But you can feel that.

We can actually go deeper into and actually resonate this code of finding my Yes to the Infinity of Intimacy that's asking me for my deepest heart's desire. We must first step out of victim identity before we can identify our unique contribution.

VICTIMHOOD IS A LIE

That's such a deep idea, and I want to relate it directly back to our code of this week. Because if I want to know what love is, I have to know that victimhood is a lie.

 Our code of this week is about knowing what my deepest *Yes* is. My deepest *Yes* is my unique gorgeous contribution unlike any other. To make my unique gorgeous contribution, I have to make that my identity. **My identity is not where I've been victimized, and it's not as a victimizer**. We have to step out of that victim-victimizer dynamic. Because remember the price of innocence—which is when we make ourselves victims and we say we're innocent—the price of innocence is impotence.

There's always a contribution system, the move from being a victim to what we call in the *dharma* a "player"—where I'm actually not on the stands, I'm on the court—is to actually look at a situation, because **in every situation, there's always a contribution system, and there's always my part in the contribution system**. I can try and figure out, this is what he/she did to me. Or I can ask, *What's my part? Where am I powerful?* I've always said this for the last decade. If I have 10% in the contribution system, I take 100% responsibility for my 10%, whatever it is. If I take 100% responsibility for my 10%, or my 50%, or whatever it is, then we forgive each other. Then we create at the next level; we create in the next way.

There's a very beautiful teaching that on the day that someone gets married, you fast, because that day is called the Day of Atonement. It's the Day of Atonement, which is the day of forgiveness. Because the day that I get married is the day I want to be more intimate than I ever was, whatever that form of marriage is. There's many ways of getting married; there's many kinds of *Hieros Gamos*. Divine marriages abound, there's whole mates all over the place; we're joining genius, we're coming together. In order to come together, I have to be out of victimhood. If I'm holding on to victimhood, that becomes my identity. My identity becomes where I feel that I was hurt. If I take myself out of the circle of power and out of the circle of responsibility, then I attach to the victimhood, and then I can't be my unique quality of intimacy; I can't be my unique gorgeousness.

We live in a world in which everyone's claiming victimhood. Identity has now become my victim identity. There was an incredible article called *The Culture of Victimization*. We have to step out of that. **I have to transform my wounds and transform them from an insult into the wounds of love.**

One of the deepest teachings of the Hindu *dharma*, that Franklin Jones loved to teach—and he teaches it particularly in Chapter 21 of his beautiful book called *The Dawn Horse Testament*—is *how do you turn the insult into the wounds of love*? We feel insulted, and we're right. But to claim a unique intimacy, to claim my unique and stunning gorgeousness, I have to give up the insult. I have to give up the power I get—because there's all sorts of subtle power I claim in being a victim. The victim's power derives and emerges from the claim of powerlessness. I have to actually claim my power, claim the integrity of my words, claim the integrity of my knowing and the integrity of my *Yes*, and stand in the full power of my beauty and my gorgeousness.

We have to hold each other accountable. We don't just hold each other accountable, we call each other out. That's what it means to love each other; to love and to offer loving critique is part of love. But I can't let my power derive from my powerlessness.

> *My power derives from the unique quality of intimacy that lives alive, gorgeously and stunningly, in me, as me, and through me.*

Giving my gift, coming together towards a planetary awakening in love through Unique Self Symphonies, where I am standing, looking at you with a good eye. We're in Symphony. We all look at each other with a good eye. Our instruments resonate with each other; we're in resonance with each other, and there's a new super-coherence of intimacy that's created on the planet. That's what we're standing for here.

We're standing for the move, as Barbara said, beyond victimization. It's a beautiful topic that's relevant to me, and it's relevant to every single one of us.

This is our moment to say *Yes*.

This is our moment to love each other deeper.

This is our moment to rip our hearts open and to scream out: *I want to know what love is*. We're going to end today's church with *I want to know what love is*, just to look at each other in the eye and sing this and chant this together—and literally love us open.

CHAPTER FIVE

YOUR EVOLUTIONARY POTENTIAL BLUEPRINT IS IN YOUR DEEPEST HEART'S DESIRE

Episode 145 — July 20, 2019

THE MINOR FLUCTUATION POINT THAT JUMPS HUMANITY TO A HIGHER LEVEL OF ORDER

Let's find our way here. Who are we? We're in Florence, and it's the Renaissance. The Black Death has just tragically swept through Europe. You can't go to every village and heal every village, because you don't have the means or the capacity. But you realize that we have to transform suffering; we have to create a better world.

So what do you do?

You do the one thing that was available—that was *the ninja move*: it was the complete transformative invitation of modernity. You tell a new story.

That's what modernity did. Modernity stepped out of premodernity, where everyone was locked in a separate, sectarian story, and each story was thought to be mutually exclusively better and true than all the other stories.

Therefore, *I had a right to start a war, to conquer, to kill and oppress you, in order that you would realize the truth of my story*. We do that in our own lives.

Modernity steps in and says, *No, there's a common story; there's a shared story*. Modernity comes in and extracts from premodernity a set of universals. **Modernity extracts from premodernity a common human narrative, and that common human narrative was called the perennial philosophy**.

The perennial philosophy made a lot of mistakes. But it was a first attempt to create a shared human narrative of what it means to be a human being. That's unbelievable! Yes, it made mistakes, and it got things a little bit confused. Often the perennial narrative would claim things as absolutely true, that were actually not absolutely true:

- It disempowered gays and lesbians.
- It disempowered certain kinds of sexuality.
- It disempowered, often, African Americans.
- It made British imperialism and colonialism the center of the world.
- It was stuck in cultural modes.
- It was trying to do universals, but it couldn't get out of its own cultural context of its own power-seeking.

It's gotten critiqued, the perennial philosophy, as being lost in too much of a cultural construction. But they got the right idea.

I'm actually now working in the next two months on reclaiming the perennial philosophy, clarifying it of its mistakes, and sharing it with the world again as part of the great gift of the church. We're going to be talking about that. But what we're doing in church is, we're moving the next step. We're moving beyond the perennial philosophy. We're correcting all of its mistakes. We're integrating all of the new knowing (the somatic knowing, the sensual knowing, the economic knowing, the political knowing) and all of the new technologies (social technologies, viral technologies, information technologies)—and we're articulating the new narrative.

The Perennial Philosophy is the best memory of our past. The person who created that name, by the way, was Leibniz. He called it the *philosophia perennis*. Then, Aldous Huxley wrote a book called *The Perennial Philosophy* summarizing that idea. The perennial philosophy is the best attempt at the great memory of our past. But the new narrative, what we're doing here in church, the new story, that's the memory of our future.

We're here to articulate a memory of the future.

We're here because just like da Vinci in Florence, we're in the 11th hour. It's not the Black Death, but it's an entire set of intensified existential risks that threaten the very core of our existence in a way that's never happened before on Earth. Because exponential tech creates exponential damage. Bows and arrows can do so much, drones loaded with nuclear payloads can do something else. There's an entire list of about ten major existential threats to Reality. Like da Vinci, after the Black Death had ravaged Europe, what do you do?

We have this Global Action Paralysis; we can't move. What we're saying here in church, and this is the intention we set every week, is that the true source of this Global Action Paralysis is a global intimacy disorder. **The global intimacy disorder is rooted in the fact that we can't find each other, and we can't find each other because we don't have a shared story; we don't have a shared narrative.**

Imagine when you're in a situation where people are fighting about what happens. So we're trying to say:

- Let's hold it all gently.
- Let's see together what is our shared view of what happened is?

- What's our shared view of Reality?
- Let's get out of our narrow perspective, and let's create a shared perspective.
- What are the great true universals that we can all hold together?

We're articulating a new story, which is the Universe: A Love Story—not an ordinary love story, an Evolutionary Love Story. Reality, driven and moved by allurement all the way up from the prehension—as Alfred North Whitehead said—that lives in molecules and atoms, all the way to the love that lives between us. Reality is driven by the desire to come close together, to create new wholes from separate parts. That's what nature has always done.

Nature, divinity, the self-organizing Universe, has always created new wholes from separate parts, which have always jumped us to a higher level of order.

But there's always been one requirement. We sometimes call it in systems theory "a minor fluctuation point." Margaret Mead talked about it; it means a group of committed people who get together. Ten thousand of us have signed up to the Evolutionary Church and said:

> We're going to be that minor fluctuation point.
> We're going to live the *dharma*.
> We're going to make mistakes, we're going to be imperfect, but
>   we're going to live the *dharma*.
> We're going to live that new reality.
> We're going to live the Universe: A Love Story.
> We're going to be not ordinary lovers, but Outrageous Lovers.

That's what our church is. We are a minor fluctuation point. We are *amor* itself. **We're radically committed to jumping the entire system—through our very being and our very loving each other—to a higher level of order; a higher level of elegant order, a higher level of freedom**. Like the African American Church in the Civil Rights Movement, which animated that entire great movement, we in the Evolutionary Church are the human rights movement; we are the global spirituality movement. We're calling ourselves One World Church, reclaiming love as religion towards a pragmatic politics of love.

IN PRAYER, WE EXPERIENCE QUIVERING TENDERNESS AND EXPLOSIVE ALIVENESS

We're going to enter into prayer. What is prayer? God is not just the Infinity of Power; God is the Infinity of Intimacy. To access that, we have to access that in first-person. What does it mean God is the Infinity of Intimacy?

Imagine, for a second, your most infinite, intimate experience. Just write a word that captures that feeling—*melting* could be the word, or *open*, or *merging*. It could be your most intimate, tender emotional experience. It could be your most erotic sexual experience—they're all parts of different dimensions of intimacy. The Divine yearns for us erotically; the Divine yearns for us tenderly.

Imagine the most intimate experience you've ever had, the one that brings love and desire together. That's always when it gets the best. It's quivering tenderness, and at the same time, it's explosive aliveness.

Bring it together. Now, exponentialize that; double it, triple it, quadruple it, ten times, twenty times. Exponentialize it! Now imagine, that's how Infinity feels about you. That's the Infinity of Intimacy, which desires the intimate. If you just got that, that is an awakened enlightened realization. It's not in your mind, it's just a glimmer. But that's an enlightened, awakened realization of the divine experience. It's a trans-conceptual disclosure, it's beyond concept. This is called a trans-conceptual disclosure, and it's trans-cultural. It's not in any culture, it's perennial—you can access it. This is the enlightened realization of Infinity in its second-person. That's what prayer is.

We're about to move into prayer. We're going to do our hymn with Leonard Cohen. But before that, we want to get what prayer is. We're going to bring it down, not just for ourselves, we're going to bring this down for all of Reality.

Because prayer has gotten lost. Prayer has become about a cosmic vending machine god who's homophobic and ethnocentric and owned only by one religion. That's not prayer. Prayer is the realization that the God you don't believe in doesn't exist. God is not just the Infinity of Power, God is the Infinity of Intimacy. That's Infinity in the second-person.

There is, of course, Spirit:, Infinity in the first-person. It's the God that lives in me, as me, and through me: *tat tvam asi*: Thou Art That. It's critically important in every mystical tradition and the interior sciences, so we realize that truth. But that's not prayer—put that aside for a second. That's meditation. That's introspection. That's contemplation. That's also the experience of Outrageous Love when I feel Divine Outrageous Love moving in me. That's first-person.

Third-person is, I feel there's an energy and a force of Outrageous Love and Evolutionary Love driving Cosmos. The Universe is a love story, and the energy driving the plotline is Evolutionary Love. That's third-person.

But now we're in prayer. This is the Holy Trinity. It's the new Holy Trinity of the One World Church: reclaiming love as religion towards a pragmatic politics of love. We have to reclaim prayer. Prayer is, I turn to Spirit in the second-person who knows my name, who is the Infinity of Intimacy. In prayer, **what I have to do is shift perspective from *mi'tzidenu*, my side, and I go to the Divine side, *mi'tzido*.** I shift perspective.

That's what we're doing in this meditation: we're shifting perspectives. I'm saying, *What does God feel like?* Because what a true interior scientist wants to know is, *How can I feel the inner face of Cosmos?* Sometimes you do a journey to find that out, other times you let yourself fall in love. But you don't want to just be seeing, you want to be stepping inside and feeling Reality from the inside.

THE UNIVERSE FEELS A DESIRE FOR INTIMACY

I want you to understand a sentence. If you forget everything we ever said to each other, understand this. It's gorgeous, and it is the absolute truth. I know it to be true, absolutely. I give you my absolute word of honor, and I stake everything on it.

The Universe feels. What does the Universe feel? The Universe feels love. The Universe feels desire. **The Universe feels a desire for intimacy, and the Universe feels a personal desire for radical intimacy with you.** I have tears in my eyes!

The Universe feels, and the Universe feels love. But it's more than that. It's not just this *agápē* kind of sweetie love. No, it's this erotic, burning, pulsing desire for union and for full knowing. Of who? You! You! You! Personally and intimately. If the Universe only knows Marc and it doesn't know you, the Universe is devastated. There's a lot of room for monogamy, but not for God; God is polyamorous.

> *God is madly in love with each one of us infinitely and personally, and knowing that is how I enter prayer.*

We're going to go into our hymn: the holy and broken *Hallelujah*. But our intention is that we're going to bring to the Divine, everything. So, we're going to bring everything to God, our holy and our broken *Hallelujah*. After we listen to the hymn and sing it together with Leonard Cohen, each in our own place, and we come together, we're going to realize that the Infinity of Intimacy is looking at me and saying: *You! You! You!* And we're going to ask for everything, because prayer affirms the dignity of personal need.

"Hallelujah," Leonard Cohen [See Appendix].

61

Hallelujah. We're going to offer our prayer. And when we pray in the dignity of personal need, we ask for everything. Let's step in and say: *I pray for and ask for everything.*

Let's just begin the prayers. Barbara is going to take us into the next step of the code. Even though she's dead, we're going to play a recording from when she was alive. She's going to talk to us about how we actually find our deepest heart's desire, which is the most intimate relationship to ourselves and to Reality.

MY DEEPEST HEART'S DESIRE HOLDS THE BLUEPRINT FOR MY EVOLUTIONARY POTENTIAL

Thank you, Marc. As you know, I've been going over this question with you all week—personally, through my own inner dialogue, deepening in prayer in a very profound way. I want to share with everyone.

Here is the question. And this is number one—there are two parts: Ask clearly and boldly for your deepest heart's desire. For in that deepest heart's desire is the blueprint of your evolutionary God-given potential. This is a very deep thing because most of us do not know our deepest heart's desire, even in our prayers. Yes, we desire what we're praying for, but I've been reading them carefully. A few of them seem to come from the deepest heart's desire, but even they don't come specifically.

Because the heart's desires are specific. They're not just *I want to be more loving*, or just a generalized desire for greater contact with God. No, ask clearly and boldly for your deepest heart's desire because in it, God has placed the blueprint of that extraordinary evolutionary potential you have that's God-given. It's one thing asking God for what we want, but it's another thing to check into what God has given us—to say yes to the God-given potential, and then act on it and see what happens. Because what happens is awesome!

First of all, to get to your deepest heart's desire, you have to be outrageous. You don't really usually let your deepest heart's desire out, even unto yourself, because it's too big, much less your blueprint of your potentials is so great that you wouldn't dare announce them. That's the reason this actually expands the prayer into a next level.

I'm going to ask, what was my deepest heart's desire? Now this is in the middle of the night and I didn't really know, and I didn't have a good clear answer until it just came up. Alright, my deepest heart's desire is to co-create a context in which *Homo amor universalis* can self-connect. I feel that *Homo amor universalis*—towards which our church is dedicated, and which is in every single one of us—is the emerging humanity, the new human and the new humanity, the new species that collectively holds the blueprints of the potentiality of life itself. I mean, that's awesome! I have to put my part in there.

I want everybody to take a moment now to ask themselves the question. When you ask clearly and boldly for your deepest heart's desire, just see that for a moment, and then you're going to ask yourself the question: what is your deepest unique potential to achieve that? I think I know yours, Marc, but I'm not even sure because you're so broad.

I'll tell you, my deepest heart's desire is to create a vehicle, like this church, probably on the internet, through which *Homo amor universalis* can actually express their blueprint of who they are and what they are creating. One moment of that on Earth will change consciousness in the entire field. That's how great we are. My blueprint of my heart's desire is: I know how to do that. I started to work on it this weekend, and I began to get revelation after revelation—particularly after going over Wheel 2.0, which I won't go into now. The more I went into it, I realized that my deepest heart's desire is my blueprint of my evolutionary potential. Then I was thinking of you, Marc, and your deepest heart's desire, and the evolutionary blueprint of your potential being exactly that.

Knowing your deepest heart's desire is awesomely revelatory, particularly if you do it with each other and if you share it with each other and keep nurturing it. Because the thing that you're saying here is that God is completely available and loves all of us—that there is no God separating any of us out. I'm taking this whole prayer the next step, which is: *God in me, as me, with unique potential.* To realize that which God has given me to yearn for is taking prayer all the way through.

Since we're living at a moment on Earth when things could go down very quickly, and as you have been saying, the suffering in the world is beyond belief, it's exactly as you say: every single person can go to their place where they're most needed to give their Evolutionary Love. The vehicle for humanity's next step that I most deeply desire to create is inherent in what you're saying.

It helped me when I realized that I know how to create an experience for humanity where this vehicle can happen. How come I know that? Because it's my blueprint. I didn't make any of it up. Nobody really makes up their deepest heart's desire or their blueprint on how to realize it. Even though we can learn a lot about how to do it, and to clarify what it is, the clarification of that desire makes it more specific and not just generalized. Like, *I want to give more love into the world*—that's too generalized. God is specific in every single realm. Look at the eye, the ear, and look at what it took to create us with 52 trillion cells, every one of them unique.

This goes through then to our uniqueness in prayer. **When I ask clearly and boldly for my heart's desire, I'm doing that uniquely**. It's my heart's desire, not somebody else's, and I have the blueprint in me. Once I say that, once I'm willing to accept it as my heart's desire, then I know that the blueprint in me is designed perfectly to realize it. It's often a desire that I almost wouldn't dare say to anybody because it's so big. I'm suggesting this is true for everybody.

WE HAVE TO INVEST HIGH TECH WITH EVOLUTIONARY LOVE

It's been an incredible few months. Barbara just passed away this past April 6th. I've said a couple of times, I have my last messages from her which basically said: *I'm going to be okay; we'll do church the next morning.*

We talked for the last two days about the future of church, and how that was going to be the center and the vehicle for everything that we need to do to articulate *Homo amor*; to bring *Homo amor* into the world and to actually realize the new story.

My friend and colleague, Yuval Harare, wrote this book, *Homo Sapiens*, and then he wrote a book about 21 Questions.

He says, *there's no story*, and because there's no story, there's the danger of dystopia of *homo deus*. *Homo deus* means not a human being who's actually a God, but the human being who is, in a grotesque way, biohacking their way to an immortality for the wealthy, where the gap between haves and have-nots expands immeasurably.

Instead of anthro-ontology (AO)—that is to say, the mysteries are within us*: anthro*, meaning human being, and *ontology*, meaning for real—we have AI. We have AI instead of AO.

We have artificial intelligence, which is driven by algorithmic computational power, which actually bypasses the face and bypasses the interior. **We have to invest high-tech with Evolutionary Love, and we have to do it by telling a new story**. Every techie, every person doing algorithms that Google and Facebook use, has to actually have a sense of: *who am I? I am an irreducibly unique expression of* LoveIntelligence *and* LoveBeauty. *I am Homo amor. I am evolution waking up to itself.* This church is essential.

ACTIVATING *HOMO AMOR* BY ACCESSING OUR DEEPEST HEART'S DESIRE

Let's step in all the way. Here we are, let's put it all together. Just to see where we are, and who we are. We are *Homo amor*; we are the new human and the new humanity. How do we take our place? We actually access our Unique Self. **My Unique Self is not my separate self, it's not my Myers Briggs test. It's the unique configuration of intimacy**. It's the unique expression of LoveIntelligence that's an expression of the entire field uniquely expressed as me.

We are *Homo amor*. As Barbara said, we are *Homo amor*, and we activate *Homo amor*. This church is the activation of *Homo amor*. This church is One World Church, which is reclaiming love as religion—but not ordinary love; Evolutionary Love and Outrageous Love—towards the pragmatic politics of love.

This church is about activating *Homo amor*. The activation process is multi-level, but one key level of the activation process is to access your deepest heart's desire. When you access your deepest heart's desire, you're accessing not your personal desire, you're actually accessing the field of the Divine. The Divine field is desire. There's a Field of Desire, and I am a unique expression of that Field of Desire. The yearning in me, the unrest in me, can't be healed by medicating it, by ignoring it, or by denying it.

That yearning and that unrest in me is Divine yearning and Divine unrest.

It's the yearning of evolution itself, awakening in me, as me, and through me. It's the desire of evolution, speaking and sprouting through the cracks in the pavement of Reality, in me, as me, and through me. My deepest heart's desire and your deepest heart's desire matter immeasurably.

All of this church is about asking a question. The question is: I want to know what love is. That's what it is. We're going to end with that prayer because we know what love is. We're going to ask it, and we're going to answer it.

Love is *Homo amor. I want to know what love is.*

"I Want To Know What Love Is," Foreigner [See Appendix].

CHAPTER SIX

POWER IS HOLY DESIRE: EVERY HUMAN HAS AN OBLIGATION TO BE POWER-HUNGRY

Episode 146 — July 27, 2019

TO RESPOND TO THE GLOBAL INTIMACY DISORDER, WE NEED A NEW STORY

I just want to say, as we go into Evolutionary Church this week, just how honored and proud I am that we have this group of people:

- We are together moving down the field.
- We are the Unique Self Symphony.
- We are activating this new human potential.
- We are potentiating the next phase in human existence.

Just to set our intention, we're at a particular moment here, and the moment is this moment which we're calling the 11th hour. That's incredibly serious. **We're in a moment in which our technology has gone exponential, with enormous positivity, but also with enormous risk**. We face for the first time in our history, what we call existential risk—meaning risk to our very existence. There are about ten major sources of existential risk.

What we've done at the Center is, we've cut through beneath the security services around the world who are looking at this in terms of scenario planning. We've cut through beneath the centers for existential risk, there are about five of them, that are thinking about this in terms of infrastructure issues. Because what I'm sure about, as sure as da Vinci was in Florence, is that the only way we can engage existential risk is how da Vinci engaged in the Renaissance, the Black Death and the tragedy that swept Europe. We have to tell a new story. Because actually at the root of our global action confusion, and our Global Action Paralysis, is a global intimacy disorder.

At the very core of everything is a global intimacy disorder, which means it's a failure of coherence; we're not in coherence. Reality naturally moves towards coherence. Then the human being comes on the scene, and Reality keeps moving towards higher and higher levels of coherence. But at the same time, there's potential for dysfunction; there's potential for open loops in a system, and open loops means incoherence.

Just to give you one little example: plastics. Plastics are an open loop. Plastics are drowning the seas, killing fish that are vital for their own being and for life itself; killing coral reefs, which we need to survive; etc. Anyone on this phone call who thinks *I am me, I'm the sum total of me* is just living in an illusion. It's bad ontology. It's bad semiotics. It's just not true. **I am an emergence of the entire system**. I can't live without plants, and plants can't live without coral reefs. The range of species we have is absolutely necessary for you and me to breathe, because we're all breathing together in a system. The system has to be a closed loop system, in which everything feeds into everything else. When we get incoherence, we have open loops in the system.

For example, we generate so many containers from plastic. But then we dump those dump into the sea, and now you have miles and miles and miles of sea with dead fish zones. Even at the same time, we've created nets that have fished the seas for 100 years in a way that we haven't done before. It took billions of years to create resources that were exploited in 100 years. We've actually made an enormous amount of life extinct, both through our fishing and through plastics. The amount of damage plastics are creating has a direct effect on our ability to breathe on the planet.

That's just one example of an open loop. We're in rivalrous system, in which there are only win/lose metrics—you're either winning or losing—that's what drives plastics. You're running a company and you're winning or losing, and you're winning or losing in your life—you're successful or unsuccessful. That's what drives plastics on every level. **It's the win/lose metrics in every department of government, between countries, and between each other, that is the core driver of existential risk.**

So, how do we respond? We need to respond by moving beyond win/lose metrics to a new system, a new vision, a new story. It's a story that's not a win-lose story. It's not even a hero's journey, where I step away from the larger structures of Reality and look for my own psychological transformation.

> *We have to move from the hero's journey to the Homo amor journey.*

We have to go from the hero's journey—which is beautiful, but it's my psychological story—and we have to integrate the hero's journey in the larger *Homo amor* journey to actually awaken as a Unique Self in a Unique Self Symphony. **I'm a unique configuration of intimacy, I'm a unique configuration of desire, and my desire is part of the larger Field of Desire.**

My deepest heart's desire, which we put at the center of The Wheel of Co-Creation, is to actually live my deepest aliveness, which comes from giving my unique gift and having the world applaud, both silently and publicly. I want to awaken as Unique Self, playing my unique instrument in the Unique Self Symphony, giving my unique gift to my unique circle of intimacy and influence, from which I draw my joy and my delight. That's what this church is about.

This church is a synagogue, a mosque, a secular humanist center, and an atheist center. **We call it a church because we want to draw on the energy of Spirit, and we want to transform all of the shadows of church into a powerful shared vision.**

We are the One World Church: reclaiming love as religion towards a practical pragmatic politics of love. Not ordinary love—Evolutionary Love. That's our intention. What a crazy intention!

THE NEW CONFIGURATION OF INTIMACY TURNS TO THE INFINITY OF INTIMACY IN PRAYER

The Evolutionary Love Code is really simple. It's a three-word code this week, which is:

Power is holy.

That's what we're going to talk about, we're going to talk about *power is holy* in relationship to *Homo amor*. We actually want to be power-hungry, and we're going to talk about what it means to be power-hungry and what it means that power is holy.

First, we're going to pray—not to the god who's a cosmic vending machine but to God who is the Infinity of Intimacy. Here's a huge sentence which changes all of evolutionary science. I was talking to Ervin Laszlo about this two weeks ago, and we just had this incredible conversation. Ervin always talks about super-coherence. I shared with Ervin: *Super-coherence is what it looks like on the outside, but what's the inside of super-coherence?* It is Reality moving—evolution having a plotline, as we call it here. It has a plotline—it's moving someplace—from simplicity to complexity. **Complexity is super-coherence, but what's on the inside of super-coherence is intimacy.**

When you hear, *Reality is moving towards more complexity and more coherence*, that's great. But what does that mean? It means Reality is more and more intimate. Reality is moving. This is a huge sentence which works across all disciplines, and it's what we're working on writing now; it's the emergence of *Homo amor*.

Reality is the progressive deepening of intimacies.

Homo amor is this new emergent, this new configuration of intimacy—this new human and the new humanity. Source, Divinity, is the Infinity of Intimacy that knows our name. How exquisite is that!

So, we turn to the Infinity of Intimacy that knows every one of us. That Infinity of Intimacy that knows our name holds us; it holds everything—holds our holy and our broken *Hallelujah*. We have to bring it all to the table, our holy and our broken *Hallelujah*.

"Hallelujah," Leonard Cohen [See Appendix].

It's so good to literally lift the prayers to the sky and to offer and bring in every prayer from around the world. *Amen* and *Hallelujah*! Now, when we pray, we open up the space in ourselves, in our hearts, because my heart is part of the one love and one heart.

There are three faces of the Divine. It's core to our *dharma*.

- God moves in me, as me, and through me; that's God in the first-person.
- God is the flowing force of Outrageous Love in Cosmos; that's third-person.
- God speaking to me; that's second-person.

My good friend Michael and I were talking about this a few years ago. Michael talks about it as: *I speak to it, I speak about it, and I speak from it.* It's the same. I speak to second-person, I speak as it as first-person, but I see it moving before me in the laws of physics as third-person. These are always happening all together.

73

WE MUST CLAIM OUR HOLY POWER *OF*, POWER *FOR*, AND POWER *OVER*

We're here now in this moment, in this Unique Self Symphony, to bring down this code. The code is: Power is holy. I'm going to add to the code.

> Power is holy, and every human being is obligated to be power-hungry.

It's so important. Power is holy, and every human being is obligated to be power-hungry. What does that mean? This is where Jimi Hendrix got it a little bit wrong. Jimmy, we love you! Whether you're a conservative or a liberal doesn't matter; we all love *Woodstock: Star Spangled Banner*. But Jimmy got something wrong. Jimmy said, *The world is going to be healed when the power of love is stronger than the love of power*. No, not exactly.

The world is going to be healed when we realize that love and power are one. Power is the animating Eros of the evolutionary impulse.

When I'm in my Unique Self, and I'm feeling the power of the evolutionary impulse moving in me uniquely, then I am filled with power, and that is the power of evolution. It's both the power *of* evolution pulsing in me, and it's the power in service and devotion *for* the sake of the whole. Now, when I feel the power of evolution moving in me and I experience the power that surges in me, to give my unique gift as a unique instrument in this larger symphony of life in my unique circle of intimacy and influence, I don't need the abusive form of power-over—the shadow form of power-over where I have power over you in order to give me a sense of existing.

I'm going to give you now the most tragic form of that abusive power-over: murder. We all experienced this great tragedy when a footballer here in America was accused of murdering his beloved because she went and left him and was with someone else. He lost power over her, so he had to assume ultimate power over and killed her. Oh my god! But we do that in a thousand ways with each other.

Of course, figurative killing is not the same as physical killing, obviously. But we go to murder each other, we go to make each other small. As the Talmud, the great mystical tradition, says: when a person's face goes white because they're in trauma—they go white because they're afraid, they go white because they're not held, they go white basically because they're not seen—*when the blood goes out of your face, it's like you were murdered.* Everyone has a seat at the table. Everyone's a Unique Self. Everyone has a unique gift. **There's no one extra on the set; no one's left outside of the circle.**

This is when I'm actually experiencing myself, not in win/lose metrics, but knowing that I'm a child of the universe, that I'm a good child of the universe, because I have a unique gift to give and a unique life to live. I have a poem to write and a song to sing that no one else who ever was, is, or will be can sing but me. That is part of my birthright as a human being.

What are we committed to here in the Evolutionary Church? Are we excited about this? We are! Are we evangelists, meaning are we bringing the Good News? We are! But not in an exclusive overwhelming, dominating way; we're overwhelmed with excitement. We have a dream! We have a dream that every human being wakes up in the world knowing:

I don't need abusive power over you to feel my power.

I'm actually power-hungry for my unique power.

I don't want your power; your power doesn't fit into me—it explodes my system and it short-circuits me.

I want to plug my Unique Self into the electricity—into the *shefa*, the *Shakti*, the *Qi*—of Cosmos itself. I want it to enliven me. But I can only be enlivened by my power, I can't take your power.

Now we can support each other, and we can be devoted to each other.

- There's power *of*, which is the unique power of evolution moving in me.

75

- Then there's power *for*, because when the unique power of evolution moves in me, I want to be in service. I'm in devotion, I'm power for the sake of all Cosmos.
- Then there's power *over*.

There's *abusive power over*, but not all *power over* is abusive, that's a wrong distinction. There's power-over that's beautiful; we all have power over each other. The second we love each other, we have power over each other. If I love you, you have the power to hurt me. If I open my heart to you, you can stab me in the chest. When God loves us madly, when the Infinity of Intimacy becomes intimate with us, then we have power over the Infinity of Intimacy. Because the Infinity of Intimacy desperately wants to be aligned and to be loved and seen and recognized, even as it recognizes and loves us.

The second we open our hearts, we surrender our power and we're vulnerable. **We all have power over each other and hold each other in quivering tenderness.**

And the power we have over each other is the beauty of power over.

There are three parts to the *dharma* of power.

> Part one of the Dharma: Power is holy.
> What's the second part? Every human being is obligated to be power-hungry.
> Part three: I'm power-hungry for my unique power, not yours. Because what does your power do? Your power short-circuits me.

There's the power *of* evolution moving in me, as me, and through me. There's power *for* the sake of the all.

Then there's the holy and broken and gorgeous and tender power we all have over each other. I was thinking about that movie, *A Star is Born*, and Bradley Cooper and Lady Gaga, in the sense of this beautiful power they had over each other that just breaks your heart open. Then there's abusive power over when I'm disconnected and disassociated from my authentic power. When my only Eros is a pseudo-eros, then I have this false dominating power over you. Now we're going to turn to Barbara, and Barbara is going to take us into power in her own words.

MY DEEPEST HEART'S DESIRE IS THE IMPULSE OF THE HOLY POWER OF EVOLUTION INSIDE ME

Yes, power is holy, and power is holy desire. Because where does our power come from, if not from that which we most deeply desire? Because it's not just external power; we're talking here about internal power.

For a moment, imagine the entire Wheel of Co-Creation, and go into the heart of the hub of the Wheel. See that core of the spiral going into the heart of the hub of the wheel into your heart. The first step in getting the power is to feel the power of the impulse of evolution as your desire, because it comes out uniquely as you. It doesn't come out as desire in general, it comes out as your deepest heart's desire. But not as a separated self lost in the field of yearning that is impossible. No. **This power is coming out in you as the impulse of creation that's creating everything uniquely in this moment—including yourself.**

Let's spend a moment going into your deepest heart's desire and experiencing it as the impulse of the holy power of evolution inside of you. I would like anyone, as you're doing this, to write : *My deepest power of desire, my holy power of desire, uniquely is...*, and say what it is. By the way, we love the new Wheel because it's got all of Marc's memes and my memes, it's a living system; we finally have it. We are putting *Homo amor universalis* across the very center of The Wheel of Co-Creation, at the hub of the wheel. When you come forward to express your holy power of desire, place it as yourself becoming *Homo amor universalis*. That happens to you through your heart's desire and holy power of desire.

Make your desire clear. Make it specific. Let the hub of The Wheel of Co-Creation tell you how it would like you to express yourself. Because holy power has to be specific. It's not: *I'm powerful in general, I'm just here.* Here

I am. How am I powerful? How is my being powerful showing up right now? It's holy because it's attempting to see the power in you. **Get in touch with your deepest heart's desire and see it as the holy power of evolution arising in you.** Because how else would the holy power of evolution arise specifically in you and me? It doesn't just arise in general: *Oh, I'm part of the powerful expression of the Divine in the universe.* No, it's in me, it's in you, it's in the Evolutionary Church, it's in all of us.

This is what I mean by joining genius. If you're really going to join genius, know that in the heart of the power of your genius is the power of holy evolution. Isn't that true? Did you create your own genius? Did you make it up one day? No, you *are* that.

That is to say, at the heart of the hub of the wheel, your holy desire for others is now being liberated for you. Often what we're designing for others is really what we have to give to ourselves in order to give it to others. You cannot give it to others without giving it to yourself.

My own deepest heart's desire is, and I am now empowered by the impulse of evolution, going through the entire spiral, from the origin of creation to us in this holy church, creating a vehicle for the power of evolution to come to us to co-create the world. I'll tell you something more about discovering your heart's desire. The closer you get to your heart's desire, the closer you get to your evolutionary blueprint of genius. Because your unique genius resides in your holy desire to create, express, and love, however you say it. In other words, in your very uniqueness resides your unique genius.

How do we contact it? How do we get it all the way out? Most of us have that blueprint of our unique potential within ourselves without ever knowing. If I let mine out the whole way, it's awesome! I mean, it's almost embarrassing, I don't do it often. But in the church, I could. I think the blueprint of my heart's desire, when I get into it, is the awakening of humanity in a Unique Self Symphony. Therefore, this means that my unique evolutionary potential is to do that. In other words, I couldn't have a deepest heart's desire for it unless I had the genius to do it.

The desire in my heart to give my gifts the whole way—which is in everybody's heart—has a blueprint inside itself that is my potential to do that, and it's uniquely mine. But I cannot do this all by myself, no matter how great I am. I need the holy power of the holy communion of the holy church. Let's contribute to the church by being the source of bringing together the holy power of each of us to come out the whole way, individually and collectively. The church itself has a collective holy power and holy desire, which is: a culture of Evolutionary Love, and a culture of co-creativity for humanity. I contribute my highest degree of resources that I can to resource the church of Evolutionary Love. Help us to resource the Evolutionary Church; your contribution makes a difference.

I'm going to add this last wonderful thought. As Kristina says, my heart's desire is for all to know the feeling of being held. Let's say, right now, in the church of Evolutionary Love, *I have the feeling of being held, as I am resourcing all of us to fulfill our heart's desire for a culture of love and creativity, in which we are fully expressed.* So be it.

When we say *church*, what do we mean? We mean *Homo amor*. We mean the Outrageous Love Revolution. We mean being power-hungry. The distinctions we did today around power are so unbelievably important— and they change something in the very source code of All-That-Is. Every single one of us: we're gorgeous, and we're going to do this. The church is going to expand, until it has literally one million people, two million people. Yes, we are going to do it, we are utterly committed.

Since Barbara passed, it's been a journey and a transition. But the promise will be kept.

CHAPTER SEVEN

CO-CREATING IN SOCIAL SYNERGY, AN EMERGENT PROPERTY OF EROS

Episode 147 — August 3, 2019

EVERY CRISIS A CRISIS OF INTIMACY IN THE UNIVERSE: A LOVE STORY

We are ecstatic. We're ecstatic because we feel the ecstatic urgency of this moment, as we literally stand poised between dystopia and utopia. By dystopia, think *Hunger Games*. Think *Blade Runner*. Think artificial intelligence replacing most of the jobs in the world, because of which the new problem is not human exploitation but human irrelevance. Think of the ten other forms of existential risk, which are risks to our very existence that have never existed in the world before.

But we don't think of that in a way that:

- We lose our ability to act.
- We lose our ability to love.
- We get lost in the crisis.
- We begin grieving the end.
- We put our heads in the sand and just go about our business as usual, as if this is just another ordinary time and this isn't a moment of essential phase shift.

No, none of the above. Rather, our realization is: *Our crisis is a birth.*

Crisis is an evolutionary driver, and every crisis at its core is a crisis of intimacy.

The response to our crisis of intimacy, which has generated a global intimacy disorder, is to restore intimacy. We restore intimacy by telling a new story. So what's the new story?

The new story is:

- Beyond premodernity. The ancient religions, as beautiful and gorgeous as they are—and as they need to hold us and inform us and animate us—were limited; they were filled with their own shadows.
- Beyond modernity. With all its beautiful dignities, this drive for the success story created a win/lose metrics disaster, and a runaway exponential growth curve which is about to fall off a cliff.
- Beyond postmodernity, which tells us that there are no stories, and that all stories are just grand narratives.

We're taking the next step. We're moving and reclaiming the shared story of humanity, which is the *Homo amor* story. **It's the awakening of every human being as a unique expression of the LoveIntelligence and LoveBeauty that is the initiating and animating Eros energy of All-That-Is, that lives in us, as us, and through us, that invites us to commit our Outrageous Acts of Love.**

Barbara and I always talked—and we had a thousand conversations just in the last year—about the continuity of consciousness. That when we pass, when we die, it's not over. We have an enormous amount of information— both in the interior and exterior sciences—which belies the notion that it's over when it's over. I have zero question, Barbara, that you're in the continuity of consciousness. I don't know the relationship between worlds, so I don't actually know if you're accessing us now or not. I suspect that you are.

But what you and I were just wildly excited about was waking up as *Homo amor*, and going the whole way in this lifetime. This Evolutionary Church, this One-World Church, is about us together going the whole way and taking responsibility—taking our seat at the table and actually declaring the new story, and then telling the new story, and going forward as evangelists. Evangelists in the sense of having the Good News—the Good News that there is a shared story, and that the shared story is woven-together parts. It is validated truths from all the great traditions woven together in a new story—a new gorgeous whole.

The core of the story is—it's not a romantic story in the kind of tinsel sense, not a kind of New Age story, not a fundamentalist story—but it's a scientific (interior science and exterior science) realization that **Reality at its core is a love story,** and that **our personal stories are chapter and verse in the Universe: A Love Story.**

That's our intention here. Just to set that intention, as we set it every week, not only for ourselves, but we're setting it for the resonant Field of Reality. The moment that we always invoke—because it's the moment we feel is at least one model of a moment that we're so close to—is what we call the da Vinci moment in Florence.

When Leonardo da Vinci, and about a thousand other people, according to Paul Tillich, engaged for realsies in the Renaissance, **those thousand people changed the course of history because they told a new story.** They couldn't go to every village and heal the Black Death, but they could tell a new story—a new story about God, a new story about the human being, a new story about men and women. That's what we're here to do—to go beyond modernity and postmodernity, and to actually tell the new story. What an honor, and what a delight!

WE ARE FIGMENTS OF GOD: COMMUNING WITH THE FIELD OF LOVEINTELLIGENCE

We're about to go into prayer. But it's not the old prayer, not the cosmic vending machine prayer to a god owned by one religion that happens to be a little bit homophobic; not that prayer, but the prayer in which we turn to the Infinity of Intimacy that knows our name. We realize in Evolutionary Church that God is not only the Infinity of Power, God is the Infinity of Intimacy, and knows each of our names.

Just imagine this for a second. But when I say imagine, I don't mean make up, I don't mean fanciful. When Feuerbach said, *God is a figment of your* imagination, Spirit answered, *But Mr. Feuerbach, your imagination is also a figment of God.*

We're not just human beings—we're *Adam*. Remember that first word, it's a biblical word. The word *Adam* in the original Hebrew means *dimeyon*: imagination. We're *homo imaginus*.

See if you can shut your eyes just for a moment, together here in the church—the synagogue, the mosque, the gathering. We use the word church because we want to claim religion; we want to reclaim religion as important—not regressive religion, but the next stage of religion, the future of religion.

Here's the meditation. Let's imagine for a second what we call here in the One-World Church: God in the third person. God in the third person means the laws of physics, the supernovas, all the laws of mathematics. The evolutionary impulse driving all of Reality—we call that third person. Billions and billions of years, and a hundred billion galaxies, all of that power, and all of that energy, and all of that driving force, and all of those infinitely complex, gorgeously dazzling laws of Reality—that's Divinity or Spirit in the third person.

All of that Spirit in third person is sitting in a chair next to you, in this moment, looking at you knowing your name, knowing everything

about you, caring about you madly. That realization is the realization of Spirit in the second person.

But we can even go deeper. Can you hear me talking? You can. How do you hear me talking? How does that happen? Well, you have ears, but it's not just the ears. If you understand the body, it's your full presence of your intelligence and intelligent consciousness that actually lives and animates your body, and one of its vehicles or one of its tools is the structure of the ear that hears. You don't hear me just with a technical ear, you hear me with your whole presence of intelligence. If your presence of intelligence can hear me talking, is your presence of intelligence split off, dissociated, separate from the larger field of presence intelligence? Obviously not. You're part of a larger field.

Now stay with this for a second. The notion that I'm not part of the larger field is an absurdity. The notion that *it's my life, that here I am, a separate self, monad, doing my thing*—that's just dumb. It's just not true. It's not who I am. If the microbiota in the soil slightly changed, my whole life either changes, gets drastically worse, or disappears. Without the coral reef, I'm not alive. Without plants, I don't even make sense. Without trees, there's no me.

> *There's not a separate self me; I am an emergent property of the entire field.*

The Field is not just a field of exteriors; the Field is animated by a driving Eros, a driving animating consciousness.

It's such a beautiful pointing-out instruction. If you can hear me through your intelligence, your LoveIntelligence, could it be that the field of LoveIntelligence doesn't hear me? That's what prayer means. Prayer means that when we speak, our speech is heard. I'm with my Beloved. It's not that my Beloved always says *Yes*, but She hears me and She holds me. The knowing that although sometimes we feel quiet desperation, there's never lonely desperation. It's not a religious idea, in the old premodern sense. But the interior structure of Cosmos is: *I'm not alone. I'm an emergent property of the entire field: the interior field of consciousness, and the exterior field.* That's who I am.

What we do in prayer is, we turn to the Infinity of Intimacy and we say: *Hold me. Hold my* holy and broken *Hallelujah; hold the whole thing.*

But I want to just offer something else before we go into prayer with Leonard Cohen, who's with us in this One World Church—just to taste it. I want to just offer you a sacred chant of David because Leonard Cohen is about to sing to us, in the holy and broken *Hallelujah*, about David—*David's secret chord that pleased the Lord, the holy and the broken Hallelujah.*

RECLAIMING THE CORE INSIGHTS BUT NOT THE HIJACKS OF FUNDAMENTALISM

Here in the church of One Love, we also want to go back to the original sources. Here's the original source of David; this is the David that Leonard Cohen is thinking about and singing about. Here's a chant of David's from the *Psalms* themselves, that actually gives you a kind of transmission—this sense of Spirit in the second-person that's here in conversation with me, and in the One World Church. In this place, we're going to invoke from science and from the interior sciences: Sufism, Taoism, Hebrew tradition, Christian consciousness. **We're going to bring all the sciences, and we're going to weave them together into a larger whole.**

Here's a transmission from David. These are the words that David wrote in Jerusalem. I'm going to do them in Hebrew, then I'm going to give you just a translation I wrote for us, which can actually give you a sense of: *I'm not alone, all of third-person divinity is looking at me, knowing my name, and loving me madly.* Here's David's words, in my original lineage tradition, So, this is a Sabbath chant:

Mizemor shir leyom ha-Shabat tov le-hodot la-Adonai.
Lehagid baboker chasdecha ve-emunat'cha ba'leylot:

To sing a song of Sabbath, it's good to sing with God.
To speak of your love in the morning,
and to trust you in the night.

Psalms 92:01–92:02

Did you feel that? Now you might ask, *Why don't we just talk about evolution? Why are we doing this?* No, let's track this. **Sixty percent of the world lives in an organized religion and has actually a sense of this Spirit in second-person.** Then we become very liberal and sophisticated and we mock it, when we shouldn't mock it.

Yes, it's gone wrong. Yes, it's been distorted. Yes, prayer has been made primitive and turned into a cosmic vending machine. Yes, there are shadows. But at the core, the fundamentalists—they're not dumb; they're not idiots. They're beautiful, gorgeous people. The fundamentalist community all over the world is holding one core realization, which is partial, but its core is true, and what's true is this realization of Spirit in the second person.

So yes, it might get hijacked: *I own this God, and I'm only saved through Christ. Only in this form of Sufism am I saved, or only in this form of Judaism.* That's a hijack, and I get that. **But we have to reclaim the core, which is this realization of Spirit in the second-person that's holding our holy and our broken *Hallelujah*.** That we're with that Spirit in second-person that knows our name, and we can say: *to speak of your love in the morning, and to trust you in the night. I trust that you, Infinity of Intimacy, are going to hold my holy unbroken Hallelujah, and you're holding it with me.*

"Hallelujah," Leonard Cohen [See Appendix].

Prayer affirms the dignity of personal need. I'm turning to the Infinity of Intimacy, and I'm saying:

You're holding everything, my holy and my broken Hallelujah.

We pray, and we ask for everything. We ask for our deepest heart's desire, because our deepest heart's desire is the desire of Reality awakening in me. I pray for myself, my personal needs and my family, then beyond my family for my larger tribe, then my larger community, and then we stand before Reality itself and we ask for everything. But don't skip the personal. **You can never bypass personal need because it's only when I honor the dignity of my personal need that I can expand.**

Let's come closer to touch and be touched. When we say to touch and be touched, the desire to touch is a basic desire of Reality. We want to touch each other emotionally. We want to touch each other spiritually. We want to hug each other in the best way, with total mutuality and total dignity. We want to touch each other intellectually. We want to touch each other existentially. But we've created a world with castes of untouchables—we're alienated from each other. That's the global intimacy disorder.

I am the Beloved, and the Beloved holds me. I am the Beloved, and I'm held by the Beloved. That's what Rumi was saying; Rumi moves between those two. I am the Beloved, and yet there's a larger field that's holding me, and that's glorious.

Let's bring this together, all of us. Let's offer it up and lift these prayers to the sky, one love and one heart together. We don't want any dogma here. We don't want any kind of claims. **We want every word we say to be grounded in the very structure of Reality itself**. That's the new story.

Oh my god, here we are! Our code for this week is: Reality needs your service. Now, that's not a tinsel claim—that's what we call an ontology. It's for real. How do I know Reality needs me? Let's go to Barbara first.

REALITY IS A SELF-ORGANIZING UNIVERSE AND YOU ARE TAPPING INTO IT

Reality needs your service. Now, what in the world does that mean? First of all, what's Reality? Secondly, what's your service and why should it be needed? All of those things are a great mystery which I would like to explore with you. What is Reality? **We are saying that Reality is the self-organizing Universe**. It's not an external God. It's not being manipulated. But there is, you might say, an innate quality in evolution itself. It is the thing itself; it isn't something about the thing, or something external to the thing. It's the thing itself. Reality is this incredible self-organizing Universe that needs your service.

Oh my god, well, what could my service be to the self-organizing Universe of the entire billions and billions of galaxies? Zeroing in on myself within the awesome extent of the self-organizing Universe, here is what I believe everyone's true contribution to Reality is.

Your true contribution to Reality
is your deepest heart's desire.

In order for you to know what your contribution is, it's not some external act. It's not even something nice that you might do for someone or for yourself—it's your deepest heart's desire.

I want to look at that for a moment to see if it's true. Let's everyone look for a moment internally. It's not easy to come up with your deepest heart's desire. Because one of the things we've discovered about *Homo amor universalis* is that all of our vocations have no lid on the top.

Our deepest heart's desire is not, *let's make a slightly better book*, or *let's do a slightly better thing over here or there elsewhere*, even though that's important. But let's say I asked myself: *Barbara, what is your deepest heart's desire?* I had to let it go the whole way to be my deepest heart's desire, and I found it's the impulse of evolution within me—desiring.

You know what's desiring inside of you and me? It's the self-organizing Universe, and the way that the self-organizing Universe inside of you expresses itself is through your deepest heart's desire. Daring to let it go the whole way, and not holding back—not only with your prayers, but with your deepest heart's desire for your service to Reality. **When you access your deepest heart's desire, you will find that you're tapping into the essence of the self-organizing Universe inside you.**

Now, that's awesome because it's unique in everyone, and needed by everyone, through everyone, for the universe. For me, it's the Planetary Awakening in Love through a Unique Self Symphony to turn on the noosphere, so that we jump through the system of breakdown to breakthrough. That's my deepest heart's desire, and everything I do, one way or another, is coded by that. It's a self-organizing Universe. Marc's deepest heart's desire is so awesome. Or Lisa's deepest heart's desire, or everybody in this church's deepest heart's desire.

Imagine, by saying *yes* to it, you're saying *yes* to the God within you. You're saying *yes* because God is showing up as your deepest heart's desire that you have to say *Yes* to. Now, here's the other thing I find about saying *Yes* to my deepest heart's desire. Coded in it is my evolutionary genius. **Coded in your deepest heart's desire is your most awesome, creative potential.**

It's what you know, that you might not even be aware that you know unless you say *Yes* to your deepest heart's desire, because it's a secret. It's too big to be noticed, otherwise you would feel even sort of, I don't know, overly-bold or not wise to say *my deepest heart's desire is to contribute to the planetary awakening of humanity.* Let's everyone think for a moment—and maybe you want to write it down—*my deepest heart's desire is...* Know that in this desire is coded your genius, your unique evolutionary potential that knows how to do it.

Here's another one of God's secrets. When Reality needs your service, it means God needs you to say *yes* to your deepest heart's desire so God can be an expression of your most evolutionary, great potential cells—so that the universe can evolve through and as each of us. Is that a good plan? If I were God, that's the way I would have thought it up. Well, that seems to be what's so.

Let's go one more step now. I'm discovering this in the CosmoErotic Universe understanding of The Wheel of Co-Creation. Because you are in The Wheel of Co-Creation—if you could imagine the spiral and the wheel—and your deepest heart's desire is going somewhere, like in health, education, or economics. But it's not going there alone, because in The Wheel of Co-Creation, from that core of the spiral is coming everyone's expression of their deepest heart's desire—where it fits best in the whole system of the shift. As I've mentioned before, Jonas Salk says, *it's not survival of the fittest, but survival of what fits best.*

In The Wheel of Co-Creation, a process that we are doing and we'll do more of in the church, I want to do a major Wheel of Co-Creation as the church. I really do, because we will then get how Evolutionary Love shows up in a church. Because you have to do it synergistically—for Reality to show up, it seems to have coded itself with the need for synergistic convergence to make the jumps. **Evolutionary jumps are never made just through great individuals alone—they're made through synergistic convergence.**

Now, just imagine for a moment that you are in The Wheel of Co-Creation, giving your gift, and Reality needs your service. It's whatever it is that's unique for you—but you're not alone in giving your gift—so is everybody else.

Not only that, but now look at the upper wing. These are the masters and these are the great creators of our time; the people who have really broken through. Some of them are no longer with us like Teilhard and Aurobindo. And then we have, let's say, a Ken Wilber—there's a source of creation embodied in that one person. Let's put all the great ones up there too, and let's put them where they sit in the realization of our service to Reality. We're going to call on all of them this time. It's the only way to get across the jump.

I was thinking about everyone who is already a great creator—they are not alone. They are surrounded by colleagues; they're surrounded by people who are reading their books, their tapes, their teachings. Get that great circle up there, and we will discover that we have the capacity to do the whole shift. That Reality needs not only your personal capacity; it needs your capacity as part of a system of which you're fitting in best. But what we haven't yet done in society, that is most needed for everyone's Reality to serve, is to create social synergy among our genius.

What happens when social synergy is created to serve Reality is that your genius is truly a direct expression of the love code of evolution. Because where else would it come from? Just allow ourselves for a moment to realize that each of our deepest heart's desire is coded with our genius, and that our genius is an expression of the evolutionary impulse of creation, or the love story of the Universe: A Love Story. It's the core. We, as the purpose of a truly Evolutionary Church of Evolutionary Love, would be an instigator of the whole system shift. Is that true? Am I being ridiculous? Or are we having a true thought here?

I will conclude this with our request for contribution. Now, the request for contribution is enormous. Because it starts out with your deepest heart's desire saying *Yes*, as a member of this church. It starts out with you being able to give your gift of your evolutionary genius within this church. It starts out with you wanting to co-create, like we're doing when we do those conversations of the evolutionary questions, and when we do our meetings, and when we do our coming together.

Let's make this church into the first place where the deepest heart's desire and unique genius of humanity shows up as a synergistic Reality for any group. It's not to say we're the only place in the world where this will show up. **We have to be one place in the world where it shows up, because all you ever need in society is to do it once somewhere well, and it's usually in a muddy pool of evolution that nobody has ever noticed.** It's not on the top of the Empire State Building at first. I want to conclude by asking people to give a contribution financially, to the realization of their own deepest heart's desire.

Because if we join genius, financially, through our own deepest heart's desires, we can be a model for others who can do the same. We can contribute to the quantum shift. That's my request, and it couldn't be more important.

In a CosmoErotic Universe, desire is holy.

Let's just feel this together. Barbara and I talked about *dharma* often. One of the reasons that Barbara stepped into the Center for Integral Wisdom, and invited me, which I was so delighted and honored to do, to be the co-chair with her for the Foundation for Conscious Evolution, is because we're telling here a new story. We're telling the story of what we call the CosmoErotic Universe. **Reality is Eros, and Eros is the desire for ever deeper contact, to find each other, and to move beyond the dissociation in intimacy.** Eros is the desire for ever deeper contact and ever larger wholeness, and serving is one of the ways I make contact; I impact. When I impact, I make contact.

Let's find that for a second. I'm going to give you just a very simple set of principles that directly complement the *dharma* of the Center and the Foundation; this *dharma* that Barbara shared so beautifully is a key piece. It's the sense that *in a CosmoErotic Universe, desire is holy.* That's one of the very important things.

Barbara had originally done The Wheel of Co-Creation, which was beautiful, and then we completely re-shifted and changed everything as we met. It's now the central Wheel—we call it Wheel 2.0. **At the center of The Wheel of Co-Creation 2.0 is desire, because desire runs everything.** Desire means it's the desire for anything, desire for any need; the desire for tomorrow, the desire for the future.

There's a huge book out in the University of Pennsylvania called *Homo Prospectus* by Martin Seligman, which points out that we're not just determined by yesterday. When my default mode network of the brain turns off, I can actually hear the call of tomorrow. But again, it's not a metaphor; that's actually the structure of Reality. *Homo prospectus* is a sister, if you will, or a brother of *Homo amor*. *Prospectus* means I'm a prospector, meaning I'm pulled by tomorrow. *Homo amor* is drawn by the memory of the future.

My deepest heart's desire is the memory of the future that calls me into the future, but we're called not just to our personal future.

The greatest challenge in the world today is to realize that my moral community is the whole planet; I can't actually isolate. **Our love lists are too short, we need to participate in the evolution of love**. It means I don't just care about me, which is beautiful, and about my family, which I totally should. But I care about my broader group, my broader tribe, and that tribe keeps expanding because my heart expands. Remember *We Are the World* (1985), by Lionel Richie, Michael Jackson, and others.

Now all of a sudden, everyone in the world is included. But not just for the duration of a concert, I move beyond the concert, and actually, what lives in me is *We Are the World*. But more than *We Are the World*; not just every human being. But actually, every animal, and every resource, and the living and nonliving world, which is all in some sense alive and sentient and delighted, we care for all of it. The truth is, caring for all of it is not noble, it's caring for ourselves. Because who am I? **I'm an emergent property of the whole thing**. I don't exist without microbiota. That's actually who I am. To suggest anything else is just bad ontology.

Let's look at each other. Let's find each other. We find each other all over the world. We come together. *How could anyone ever tell you that you're anything less than beautiful? How could anyone ever tell you that you're less than whole? How could anyone not notice that our love is just a miracle, and how deeply all of us madly love each other?*

"How Could Anyone?" Libby Roderick [See Appendix].

Here's our sentence—the last sentence, which we'll come back to. I've been working with this sentence all week: *I'm willing to take responsibility to be an imaginal cell.* Those are the imaginal cells in the moment in which a caterpillar is about to become a butterfly. In this One-World Church, we are the imaginal cells.

I'm willing to take responsibility to be an imaginal cell for the sake of the whole, together.

CHAPTER EIGHT

WE ARE THE POSSIBILITY OF POSSIBILITY THAT GENERATED THE BIG BANG

Episode 148 — August 10, 2019

WE ARE LOOKING AT A SHARED HORIZON

Let's set our intention. You are, we are, all of us are needed. We can't do this without each other. We're so afraid of being codependent, aren't we? Here, we realize that when I say *I love you*, we also mean *I need you*. But not co-dependently—not because I have no center, not because I'm covering up my own emptiness. But because I'm so full and delighted and aware of the inner structure of the Intimate Universe, in which no one is separate, and all of us are an interdependent and inter-intimated expression of the All emerging through us. **We are all unique emergents of the whole.** The thought that I'm living my own life—that's just bad ontology. That's just dumb, it's just not true. I realize that I'm not alone, and I realize that I'm part of the whole and I can impact the whole.

What's our intention? Here in the One World Church, or the church of Evolutionary Love, where ten thousand of us have signed up from all around the world, our intention is to participate together in the evolution of love. Our intention is to awaken as *Homo amor*. We understand that

97

Homo amor is what we call the CosmoErotic Universe in person. Beloved Barbara, we're doing this together and we're doing it together every week. We are together—the CosmoErotic Universe in person. We are not joining genes, we're joining genius.

We're not just role mates, which is gorgeous, and raising kids, which is stunning. We're not just soul mates, which is beautiful, looking in each other's eyes. We've actually gone to the third level, which can include one and two, but we're whole mates. **We're looking together at a shared horizon, and we are taking responsibility for the whole story.**

So, friends, welcome. *Homo amor*, welcome. We're here to participate together in the evolution of love.

> I am *Homo amor*.
> I am the universe awakening in person.
> Evolution awakens in me.
> I'm personally implicated in the entire story, and I am powerful.

Not power over in an abusive way. But the reality is that the *power of* transformation moves through me, the *power for* the whole moves through me, and I also have *power over* the whole. Because that's what it means to be alive. I want to use that power tenderly, audaciously, and gorgeously.

GOD IS BOTH THE INFINITY OF INTIMACY AND THE LOVE THAT ANIMATES COSMOS

What's our one word? *Hey Brother*, that great song by the DJ, Avicii—that we've been singing all week. Our one word is *amor*: love. But by *amor*, we don't just mean ordinary love, which is love in exile—love exiled to only romantic love, with one particular person or one particular form, which feels a particular way, that I have for a short time and I spend my life desperately trying to recover. No, that's not *amor*.

Amor is the love that drives and animates Cosmos itself. When I access that love, and that love awakens in me, and that love moves between us, that's a love I can hold. That's a love I can renew. That's a love that can get deeper and infinitely richer and more ecstatic and more beautiful. That's the love we're talking about, *amor*.

Friends, let's enter to the Inside of the Inside together. We are before prayer. When we pray, what are we doing? We're setting now our resonant intention to participate together in the evolution of prayer, which is the evolution of God. We have to be heretics in the old church. When we talk about God:

- We're not talking about the god owned by one religion.
- We're not talking about the god who says, *I'm going to tell you exactly what to do every moment and what's right and what's wrong.*
- We're not talking about the god who is the creative source outside of Cosmos, and all of Cosmos has but to be obedient to that god to please him/her.
- We're not talking about what we call the ethnocentric cosmic vending machine god, where you put in a prayer and get out a shiny car. It doesn't work that way.

Reality is so much deeper and so much more beautiful.

We're speaking to the God who's not only the Infinity of Power, but the Infinity of Power that's inherent in Reality. God, who's the creativity, but who's also the creative force inherent in Reality; the inherent ceaseless creativity of Reality. We're talking to God—and this is the essence of prayer—who's also the Infinity of Intimacy. We turn to the Infinity of Intimacy.

Imagine your most intimate moment, most tender, most filled with aliveness, most throbbing and pulsing with goodness and lust in the best sense. That raw desire—that raw desire to be good and to be tender, that raw desire to be received, that raw desire to penetrate in the most holy and wondrous context—all of that—imagine your most stunning moment of that kind in your life, and then double it. Triple it. Times ten, and times

20, and times 100, and times 100,000, and times a million, and times 10 million. Exponentialize your most wondrous experience of both quivering tenderness and raw desire, and you'll get a sense of how the Infinity of Intimacy looks at you.

I PARTICIPATE IN THE CONSCIOUS INTELLIGENCE THAT MOVES THROUGH THE WHOLE FIELD

We do this meditation or some version of it every week in church, and we ask a question. We ask, *well, could I hear David talking?*

We say, yes, of course. I heard David talking.

Well, how did I hear David talking?

Well, because I have ears. But it's not just physical ears, it's my intelligence; the intelligence of my system. It's my conscious intelligence, moving through the physical structure of my ears, that heard David talking. The conscious intelligence of Marc heard David talking.

But one second. Is my conscious intelligence separate, discrete from, isolated from, dissociated from, the larger field of conscious intelligence?

Does conscious intelligence reside in Marc?

Well, yes. But obviously, it doesn't reside exclusively in Marc. Conscious intelligence moves through the whole field, which is why it lives in David and Barbara, and all of us; there's no one it doesn't exist in. It's powerful. **We're each a unique expression of LoveIntelligence.**

When I first shared some of these pieces of *dharma* with Barbara on the evolution of intimacy and the Possibility of Possibility, Barbara would then share that *dharma*, but in her own tone and her own way. It was my job to share it the way I shared it, and then Barbara received it, and then she would talk about the evolution of intimacy in her tone and her story. Each of us would reach different people, because that's of course the way it goes. We each have to give our gift. **We each have to stand in the uniqueness of our integrity, and the uniqueness of our gorgeousness, and the uniqueness of possibility.**

We turn to the Infinity of Intimacy, right now in this moment, that knows our name, that says: *Hey, it's great to see you; it's so good to see you.* That's what the Infinity of Intimacy says. We come before the Infinity of Intimacy and we actually offer up everything. The Infinity of Intimacy says: *I want to know everything about you. I want to know about your holy and your broken Hallelujah.* Take us inside to our weekly hymn in Evolutionary Church, the holy and broken *Hallelujah*, and bring it before the altar of the Infinity of Intimacy and we offer it all up.

"Hallelujah," Leonard Cohen [See Appendix].

Hallelujah! Hallelujah means two things in the original language. It means *hallel*: pristine praise. But *Hallelujah* also means *holelut*: drunken intoxication. It's the holy and it's the broken *Hallelujah*; it's both of them together. **There is no person who doesn't have in their lives a holy and a broken *Hallelujah*.** The way we pray is we bring it all to the Infinity of Intimacy. We go to pray and we to turn the Infinity of Intimacy, and we ask for everything because prayer affirms the dignity of personal need. We're excited about it; we're not embarrassed to be excited about it. We're excited about this new world in which I'm actually held and Reality knows my name.

Let's find it together, our song: "I Want To Know What Love Is." That's what we're praying for. We're praying that we want to know what love is. Let's just pray for this together, that the whole world knows what love is.

Love is not ordinary love. Ordinary love is beautiful, but it's too limited. It can't just be between you and me. It's got to be the Outrageous Love, the Evolutionary Love that drives everything that lives between us.

THE EVOLUTIONARY GOD IS THE POSSIBILITY OF POSSIBILITY

Evolutionary Love Code:

> The evolutionary God is the Possibility of Possibility.
>
> Evolutionary integrity is faithful to the memory of the future, even as it is faithful to the memory of the past, and it's always living in the infinite eternity of the present moment, which contains all past and all future in its transformative crucible.

Let's take it all the way home. Barbara and I are going to mix our sermons today, and we're going to actually open up an image which is a stunning and wondrous image. It's beautiful. If we can feel this, we can actually change and we can take it all the way home.

Here we go. Our code is: *the evolutionary God is the Possibility of Possibility*.

For years, I've tried to feel into how we can transmit and share the living Reality of an Intelligent Divine Consciousness that lives everywhere. It lives in me, and it lives in every one of us uniquely and wonderfully. But what is the nature of that consciousness? One part of it is intimacy and yearning. **The infinite yearns for the intimate**. There's this Infinity of Intimacy.

But there's a second dimension, which is possibility. It's what I like to call the Possibility of Possibility. Imagine that the closing off of possibility is what stands against my emergence as *Homo amor*—what stands against the divinity which is the possibility of goodness and truth and beauty. The possibility of every child knowing that they have a life to live, and a gift to give, and a poem to write, and a song to sing, because each child and each human being is a uniquely gorgeous expression of the infinite Field of Possibility.

Each of us is the Possibility of Possibility. But to really get what that means, we actually need to understand, and ask: *how did we get here?* We got here because we started at this moment where the world became recognizable as we know it, which is called the Big Bang. But the Big Bang contains within it the seed of unfolding; the seed of virtually infinite emergence. The Big Bang isn't like, *wow, where'd it come from*?

The Big Bang contains everything:

- All the laws of math.
- All the laws of physics.
- The ability to manifest a chlorophyll molecule, more complex and stunning and dazzling than all the supercomputers in the world can possibly manifest.

Yet, these were manifested by the Big Bang at particular stages of evolution, way before there's a human neocortex. How did that happen?

There's an intelligent Reality that's fully intelligent and fully conscious, that's then unfolding—the Possibility of Possibility is unfolding.

Go back to where all we had was, for example, quarks. From quarks, who do we get to? We got to everything. We got to all of us, each of us with 37.2 trillion cells. We got to a world of dazzling, gorgeous, stunning, intimate consciousness and complexity; all the laws expressing and manifesting— all from a quark.

HOMO AMOR IS THE POSSIBILITY OF POSSIBILITY

Go back before everything. Imagine, here I am at the moment of the Big Bang, and you feel the Big Bang, this great flaring forth. It's actually a flaring forth of possibility. That possibility, which contained within it the Possibility of Possibility, brought us to today.

What does that mean? **That means that right now, in this moment, we are also the Possibility of Possibility.** Just as the original quark could manifest human beings building hospitals and taking care of their weak, human beings writing poetry, and human beings emergent as *Homo amor*, we could go, as we always say, from mud to Mozart, from bacteria to Bach. We could go from *Homo sapiens* killing each other to cosmocentric intimacy, where we care about every human being, and we care about every species, and we take responsibility for the planet. How did that happen? That's the Possibility of Possibility.

What does that mean? That means that we now, in this very second, are before the same Possibility of Possibility. We face a crisis, a crisis of existential risk, a crisis of actually destroying our own habitat, because our possibility of imagining exterior technology is not matched by our possibility of imagining interior technology. We've created the power to destroy the world; we've developed through technology the power of ancient gods, but **we have no story or narrative equal to our power. We have no interior innovation or interior creativity.**

The whole thing could fall apart, and we think there's nothing to do. What do you mean, there's nothing to do? We are the Possibility of Possibility. *Homo amor* is the realization that the Possibility of Possibility is not over; it's just beginning right now. Barbara is going to talk about this from her perspective.

IMAGINE THE INFINITY OF POSSIBILITIES BEFORE THE BIG BANG

The evolutionary God is the Possibility of Possibility. To really understand that, place yourself before the Big Bang. I mean, there was a *before the Big Bang*. There was the Possibility of Possibility. There may not be just one Big Bang; there may be multiple universes, but there is a *before*. Place ourselves before that to actually absorb the awesome Reality of The Infinity of Possibility.

Okay, now take yourself up our own spiral of 32.7 billion years, and see if you can actually imagine the Infinity of Possibility before the first quark.

Here comes a quark, so you have to be really excited about the quark. Imagine the Infinity of Possibility before the first cell, before the first multicell, before the first animal, before the first human, and now here we are humans at this threshold of the Infinity of Possibility.

If we want to realize what that might mean, we have to go back to all the past infinities of possibilities—to imagine the awesome reality of such an infinity of possibilities. I'm going to make a few suggestions here. Let us stand at the basis of the sixth mass extinction on planet Earth. Let us stand where the species are dying, where we are destroying them, where we are destroying our environment, and we have the powers of gods in our nuclear and other high-tech geniuses. We have the ability for a mass extinction the likes of which you've never seen. However, it seems to me that it's always absolutely true that we are at the threshold of *Homo amor universalis*.

Now, let us assume that the Infinity of Possibility in a species called *Homo amor universalis* is as great an infinity as it was for that first cell, or that first multicell, or that first animal, or that earliest human. That the mass extinction upon which we sit is based on the misuse of power (to some degree, not entirely, nature also *extincts* things all the time). By the way, nature does not mind *extincting* things. It is not the least bit careful about keeping everybody alive. It's not like we haven't had mass species extinctions. Nature is good but not nice, in the sense of, *Oh, you're here, so we'll keep you alive no matter what.* The answer is no! You might be alive in other lifetimes, and so forth. But no, this is for real.

I am going to make a really amazing statement that I just thought of. What if the church of Evolutionary Love, which we're calling ourselves, could be the church of mass evolution? If we are at the threshold of mass extinction and the church of Evolutionary Love is founded for this purpose, could we see—not only with our personal prayers, but by thinking of ourselves as the Infinity of Possibility in every one of us? **What would it be like if we realized that at the threshold of mass evolution or extinction, the Infinity of Possibility is as great at this moment as it was when we came**

out of the Big Bang? I mean, if we're really going to take this seriously, we have to say it existed in every one of those passages—and it's still here.

I'd like to explore just for one moment what would be the infinity of possibilities at the threshold of mass evolution within our church. At the time of the early Christian church it was for the Second Coming of Christ, and that moved the entire world. Well, was it unrealistic? Actually, it was super realistic. You know why it was so super realistic? Because it changed the world.

It's super realistic. I am suggesting that we could be that super realistic about the Planetary Awakening in Love through a Unique Self Symphony. If we could be coming from the genius code of the awakening of the entire humanity to a new human, which is what they actually thought would happen for the Second Coming of Christ. Well, I think it's really Christ, because Christ was going to come again and change the world. Let us say that we are coming again to change the world.

I want to check in with everybody. I want to see if you can check in for the Infinity of Possibility within yourself as part of this church, as well as an individual, because I'm really saying it has to be a mass evolution now. If we take that phrase seriously, what does joining genius mean at the threshold of mass evolution? Oh my god, think of what that means! **Christ is coming again through the individual; the new Christ is multiplied, coming again to change the world.** *Halle-nu-yah.* Yes, planetary awakening in the church of mass evolution.

Let's just imagine for a moment, the planetary awakening in love through a Unique Self Symphony. Meaning, every single one of us is in a church launching this. Now, that's as big as the people who went into the lion's den for God—they actually walked out there and got torn to pieces. I could not ever have been that brave. But how brave is it now to do what we're doing? I don't know that I would call it brave. I would call it incorporating the possibility of all possibilities as God within you. What this is, is the incorporation of the God of all possibilities as the possibilities of God as you. That's what it is!

Now, if you can feel what that is, I'll do it for this moment for myself. I am incorporating the God of the possibility of all possibilities as me. You know what that does? It completely takes the top off the lid of your genius code. I've tried this out recently—which is to say, in groups of people, where suddenly I do this. **I am infinitely possible, as are you, to create this infinite potential future**. The reason the God of all possibilities is inside of each of us is that the future that we are creating, the God of the possibility of all possibilities has never gotten near it before. Because this is the generation—if I may say so, for the incarnation of the God of All Possibilities. We have the power of gods.

Why do you think we got all that high technology? Why did we get artificial intelligence and nanotech and biotech and quantum computing and robotics, and so forth, plus the infinity of the possibility of God within us? We are that! I now take, for the church of Evolutionary Love, all those high techs into our hearts. **Instead of excluding them, I bring high technology into the possibility of all possibilities so that we can heal the Earth**; we can free the people, we can feed everybody, we can overcome disease, we can actually reach out into the universe of billions of other planets.

We can right now invite other life, to say: *Oh, look what's happening on planet Earth!* Through the church of mass evolution, we may be even getting ready to say *hello*. If we're not alone in the universe, folks, what would it take for us to experience that together? I don't mean just individual little moments that some people have, I believe it's a whole thing. I think that this is the moment of the mass awakening of planet Earth, to be receptive to the fact that it's being born into a universe filled with life.

OUR CONTRIBUTION ALLOWS US TO STAND FOR THE EVOLUTION OF LOVE

So, we contribute everything that we possibly can to the greatest event that has never happened before. I believe it's true that the contribution to this church, which is the very first place on Earth that's actually celebrating this possibility, there's nothing compared to this, except the very earliest church. Therefore, let your contribution truly be as much as possible. But it's more than that. Let it be your life. Let it be *re*-sourcing you, *re*-sourcing yourself, and let this church do something through these contributions. I want to see how we use these contributions to reach the world. This is my life. This is my commitment. This is my contribution. Let's give it all.

Let's give it all. **Our contribution actually allows us together to raise this up to the sky, to actually create this Evolutionary Love revolution, and to stand for the evolution of love**. To stand for the church of Evolutionary Love, the One World Church, to be the Possibility of Possibility:

- The possibility of goodness, truth, and beauty.
- The possibility of no one being left out of the circle.
- The possibility of taking the shadow back and integrating it into ourselves.
- The possibility of every human being realizing *I am needed by All-That-Is, and my joy, and my creativity matters. I deserve to be loved, and now that I know that, I can actually take it in and love it open.*

So, friends, let's look each other in the eyes, around the world. This is the Outrageous Love Revolution. We are together. We are one love, and we are one heart. Sometimes people say to me: *Marc, why are you so excited about this?* I want to say it again: We're excited about it, we're passionate about it, because we know that the telling of this new story, the story of the evolution of intimacy—in which every human being has a name and a face, and beyond the facial recognition of artificial intelligence, we actually recognize each other, we choose each other, we desire each other, we need each other—we know that this is the response to suffering.

We live in a world of outrageous pain, and the only response is Outrageous Love.

CHAPTER NINE

A HUMAN BEING IS A UNIQUE WORD IN THE COSMIC SCROLL

Episode 149 — August 17, 2019

WE INVEST HIGH TECH WITH EVOLUTIONARY LOVE BY TELLING A NEW STORY

We're going to talk today about sentences. What we're doing together is we're literally reweaving the very source code of Reality. **The source code of Reality is made up of information: sentences strung together, configurations of energy and intimacy.** We need a new set of memes. Yesterday I was in Florence, in the footfalls of da Vinci, my beloved friend. As we say every week when we set our intention in this One World Church, in this church of Evolutionary Love, in this church of *Homo amor*, in which we step forward in this breach—in this moment between utopia and dystopia. This is the moment in which we could either bring to bear outrageous beauty, heaven on Sarth, in a way that we've never imagined and never thought possible, or we stand before outrageous pain of a kind that's virtually unimaginable.

In this moment, what can change the entire trajectory is to do what da Vinci did in Florence with about a thousand other people in the Renaissance, which is to tell a new story. That's what we're about, we're telling a new

story. But when we say telling a new story, the new story is not dogma—it's what we call *dharma*. We're giving the word a new meaning; we're taking this flask of *dharma* and pouring new wine into it.

By *dharma,* **we mean the best integration of the deepest validated insights of premodernity** (up to the Renaissance), **of modernity** (from the Renaissance till the mid-60s), **and then of postmodernity—all three of which had important insights**. We're weaving them together in a new synergy, in a new whole, in what we call a new configuration of intimacy greater than the sum of the parts.

Where are we? What's our intention? We're at a moment in which existential risk—a risk to our very existence—can take down the planet. We're in a moment where people have their heads down. Everyone's involved in their own individual life, maybe doing some philanthropy, maybe running an organization—maybe running their profession, taking care of their family—which are all gorgeous things to do.

But at this moment, we have to take our seat at the table of history, as we are going through a phase shift in history. This phase shift in history, as Barbara and I have said time and time again, and shared together, is like the movement from single-celled to multi-celled life. It's that significant. It's not a detail. Everything's changing, and it's going to change exponentially. When you're thinking linearly, one step after the next, you can't see it. But it's all changing exponentially; we're at a phase shift in history.

In this phase shift in history, the single most important thing we can do is invest in the source code: the source code of nanotech and biotech and infotech, the source code of the interior structures.

What's happened is our exterior imagination—literalized in technology—has run away from our deepest self.

- ◆ Our exterior imagination literalized in technology is driven by good humans—but good humans who are driven by entrepreneurship, in the sense of profit.

- ◆ It's driven by scientists seeking to create for the sake of creation.
- ◆ It's driven by greed, with no overarching sense of the impact of what's happening.

The result is actually unbelievable. The result is that no one's voting on anything important. There's no collective intelligence at play. There are runaway pockets that are developing technologies so fast that everything's changing in a way that will rid jobs from the world; most human beings won't have jobs. It's changing everything in a way in which we'll create a caste system, in which we'll have an augmented humanity. Imagine *Blade Runner*. Imagine some version of *X-Men*; highly developed artificial intelligence— able to outstrip humans even in their Unique Self mutant capacities, which is what the *X-Men* is about—that function is based on algorithmic analysis of Reality.

The core structure of what a human being is:

- ◆ Core aliveness
- ◆ Core Eros
- ◆ The core delight of being face to face
- ◆ The move towards intimacy
- ◆ The affirmation of the unique creativity of every human being beyond what their job happens to be

All that is literally on the brink of being lost.

We live in a win/lose metrics world with a complicated system which is vulnerable to radical, fragile breakdown in every second, and no one's noticing.

But we're not decimated, and we're not devastated, and we're not paralyzed. We're actually excited; we're energized by this moment, by this 11th hour. Because there's a possibility here. It's what we said last week: it's the Possibility of Possibility.

At this moment in history, we can invest the high-tech and nanotech and biotech with Evolutionary Love, with the vision of Homo amor.

We can invest the algorithms with face, with depth, with interiority, with the ontology and the mysteries that live within us, downloaded throughout Reality, as the *dharma* invests and shapes the world of technology. We can articulate and tell a new story.

Friends, we are da Vinci. I'm here in Montescudaio[3] right now with Ervin Laszlo. We're not just getting together to say hi, although we love saying hi, and we say hi with Outrageous Love. We're here together to talk about how we can join source codes together, and how we can tell a new story. Everything, all the delight, all the joy, all the beauty, all the gorgeousness, it all hangs in the balance. It's ours to do!

BARBARA IS WITH US IN THE CONTINUITY OF CONSCIOUSNESS

I remember I was talking to Barbara, and literally, as I was talking to Barbara, we were in the middle of a conversation, and I said, *let me write.* I started writing, and this code came down, and we're so excited about it. Barbara and I talked about our sermons this week. It's going to be a beautiful week.

Now, a couple of people have written to me and said, *it's so beautiful that Barbara is with us* in church. But a couple of other people wrote to me and said: *Listen, Marc, it's beautiful that you miss Barbara, but she passed away*

---

3 Montescudaio is a picturesque hilltop village located in the province of Pisa, Tuscany, Italy. Nestled in the Val di Cecina, it is approximately 15 kilometers from the Tyrrhenian Sea and is recognized as one of "I Borghi più belli d'Italia" (The Most Beautiful Villages of Italy).

three months ago, and we keep having Barbara in church. *Like, how long are you going to do this?*

Let me tell you how long I'm going to do this. For a couple of years! I'm delighted to have Barbara with us, and Barbara is delighted to be here.

Barbara and I talked often about the continuity of consciousness—I have tears in my eyes—and we said that we're going to continue doing this. Continuity of consciousness means that life is not over when it's over. **When we leave the body, we don't leave life; we leave a certain kind of participation in this realm**. But what allows a person to continue is that *we're held*. It's not over when it's over. Barbara is with us. She's playing with us, I feel her, and I look forward to having her with us deeper and deeper.

My next five years is about writing a Great Library, and one set of those books is going to be with Barbara.

I'm completely committed, the promise will be kept.

Barbara is with us. Let's sing it together, *Amor*, which means love. *Its insides are lined with love*. Not ordinary love. As in the Song of Solomon, *its insides are lined with love*.

ALLUREMENT IS THE ULTIMATE PERSONHOOD OF COSMOS, THE INFINITY OF INTIMACY

What drives Reality? What drives Reality is allurement; allurement between two quarks. You can actually feel the allurement.

We're now setting our intention for prayer. What does prayer mean? **Prayer means we live in an Intimate Universe—an Intimate Universe in which there's allurement.**

Now, there are trillions and trillions of quarks in all of us, quarks all the way up and all the way down. Meaning we're pulsing with Eros; we're pulsing with allurement. That's who we are. When we want to know how that sounds, we listen to the music from the *Phantom of the Opera*, as she's allured to go inside because he's calling her. He is always calling She, and She is always calling He; that's allurement all the way up and all the way down the evolutionary chain.

But that allurement is not just a gravitational force, it's not just an impersonal force. Allurement is ultimately unique and personal.

Allurement is the ultimate Personhood of Cosmos, the Infinity of Intimacy, which is what we call here in the One-World Church of Evolutionary Love—which is a synagogue, a mosque, and an atheist center, all of it together—God in the third-person:

- All of the forces of physics and chemistry.
- All of the grandeur.
- All of the supernovas.
- All of the Infinities of Power, of all of the universes, not one or two or a billion, but a 100 billion universes into the multiverse.

All of that power is sitting in a chair—the infinity of personhood, the Infinity of Intimacy, knowing your name—and loving you intimately and personally.

I want to introduce, we've done it once or twice, just a chant, and we'll record it so we'll have it in church. It's really a simple chant. Because we do the church on the seventh day of the week, which in the classical Hebraic tradition is the Sabbath. Here's a beautiful chant, which is going to take us into prayer.

Mizmor shir leyom ha-Shabat tov le-hodot la-Adonai.
Lehagid baboker chasdecha ve-emunat'cha ba'leylot:

To sing a song of Sabbath, it's good to sing with God.
To speak of your love in the morning,
  and to trust you in the night.

Psalms 92:01–92:02

That's prayer. Prayer is *to speak of your love in the morning and to trust you in the night*. It's the word between the Infinity of Intimacy, the Divine voice in you and me, and it's the voice between us. When we hear that voice, we can bring our holy and broken *Hallelujah*. We can bring everything to that Infinity of Intimacy that desires us, that knows our name, that yearns for us.

That's the holy and the broken *Hallelujah* that lives in each of our lives and each of our stories and each of our voices. Hallelujah," Leonard Cohen [See Appendix].

Hallelujah! Let's ask for everything, because prayer affirms the dignity of personal need. We've all come together and we're here to build a new movement. But we have to learn to pray; we have to learn to ask for everything.

We lift our prayers to the sky, and we invite them to reweave the very source code of Cosmos itself. We're going to hear from Barbara, and we're going to step into our code. This code is wildly important and exciting.

SENTIENCE IS THE SENTENCES OF REALITY WEAVING A LOVE STORY

Evolutionary Love Code:

> Sentience is not less than the sentences of Reality weaving a love story.

> Each sentence is woven by words.

> Each human being is a unique word in the cosmic scroll.

> Each word is composed of distinct letters. Each letter is a different voice that lives in the person.

> Integrated together, those different voices constitute the unique word, the unique quality of intimacy, and the unique purpose of that person's word in the Universe: A Love Story.

115

Let's read this code together. Then we're going to hear from Barbara, and then we're going to pray. *I want to know what love is.* We have so much to do—we have miles to go before we sleep today, for the evolution of love.

Here's the code: *sentience is not less than sentences of Reality weaving a love story.* Barbara, do you remember this code when we brought it down? *Each sentence is woven by words. Each human being is a unique word in the cosmic scroll. Each word is composed of distinct letters, and each letter is a different voice that lives in the person. Integrated together, those different voices constitute the unique world, the unique quality of intimacy, and the unique purpose of that person's word in the Universe: A Love Story.*

Let's feel this. I'm going to speak very briefly, and I want to hear Barbara—we're going to be saying and weaving the same sermon, the same vision together. One voice, not joining genes but joining genius, not to procreate but this time to co-create. We're moving in the world of overpopulation, in a world which is bloating itself. We're moving from joining genes to procreate, which is holy and beautiful, to the next level. We don't leave the old level behind; children are gorgeous. I have four gorgeous kids. **But we're now moving, not just to be soul mates but to be whole mates, to come together for the sake of the whole, and to be willing to say to each other:**

Let's together take responsibility to be imaginal cells, to be Outrageous Lovers, for the sake of the whole. That's our sentence.

Let's together take responsibility to be Homo amor, together as a unique We, for the sake of the whole, to be whole mates.

So, Barbara, we're whole mates today, and we're joining genius.

What does this code mean? It means that each one of us has a unique voice, and that unique voice is desperately needed in the symphony of Cosmos.

There's an orchestra, there's a symphony of evolution. There's a self-organizing Universe. For years, I've tried to share this very simple idea that science at its leading-edge always offers up a word in the place of divinity, as does the world of media, and as does the world of literature. For example, in the largest blockbuster movie *Star Wars*, we talked about the third face of God—the force that moves in Cosmos—as *The Force. May the Force be with you.*

In the leading edges of evolutionary science, we talk about the self-organizing Universe, which is the notion that Reality brings together and weaves together separate parts to form larger wholes, that the trajectory of evolution is the evolution of intimacy. **Evolution is the progressive deepening of intimacy**. If you're not jumping out of your seat when you hear that idea, even if we've talked about it thirty times in church, it's like: *wow, we've already said I love you, why say that again?* No, it's wildly fundamental, earth-shattering, and changing.

Intimacy means when two parts come together to create a shared identity, a shared Eros, a shared whole greater than the sum of its parts—when unique voices come together, when unique words come together.

In this church of mass evolution and this church of changing the source code, each of us is a word. **When we love together, our words are allured together, and our words form a sentence**. When our sentences come together, we form a paragraph, and we begin to write the new book of evolution—we begin to write the new Book of Life. Our words have energy. Each person is holding a word, and each person is holding a sentence.

Think about that for a second. We talked about the false core sentence—sentences like:

- I'm too much.
- I'm not enough.
- I'll always be alone.
- I'm not good.
- I'm broken.
- I'm an imposter.

Those are false core sentences.

But there's also the sentence which is my sentence in the source code of All-That-Is. **That's my Unique Self: it's my unique letter in the cosmic scroll**. It's my unique sentence in the cosmic scroll.

Barbara, let me turn the word to you and invite you with delight to talk just beautifully about this code. This code is about this new sentence, and *that sentence is alive; the sentence is sentient, it's alive. The sentence and the words hold living Eros and energy.*

WE'RE AT A MOMENT OF RADICAL NEWNESS ON AN EVOLUTIONARY SCALE

I'm going to start out with a poem based on the code, because I love the code today. If you remember: *sentience is not less than the sentences of Reality weaving a* love story.

Here's a little poem before my sermon. This whole code is an expression of the Unique Self Symphony, which is all the codes of all the humans guided together towards a planetary awakening in love—that this entire lineage is moving toward a quantum jump of evolution. But what makes this different from any past lineage is that they all were preparing for something, but *this lineage happens to be born at the crossover point of evolution.*

Not because we're better or smarter than the ones that came before us, but because *we're born within a small period of years, all of us in our lifetime, either going down towards further devolution or upward toward newness,* because we have not seen the next stage of evolution yet.

We really need to bring this forward about the lineage. **We're at a moment of radical newness on an evolutionary scale.**

The reason it's a new evolutionary code is because it's a new evolutionary moment for humanity. As far as I know, there's no other lineage being made for this radical newness, and it probably has to take all of them into it. I have a few poetic statements to make out about it here.

Each of our voices is amplified and glorified by being sounded in the orchestra of evolution. There is a new word frame here. Who's orchestrating this? I like the phrase: *it's the orchestra of evolution itself.* **The mighty process of creation, from nothing at all to everything that was, is, and will be, is now expressing itself through our unique sentence of Reality.**

I don't like to say our generation is more important than anyone that ever came before us—but I will, because of the weightiness of being at a cross-over point of evolution, where the balance is so sensitive to which way it goes.

Everybody in this church, who is placing the weight of their sentence of Reality in the orchestra of evolution, is 10,000 times more important to evolution than if we were doing it before the shift point. Everything that came before it is that.

What then is your sentence of Reality? Feel it coming from the source of your being, this is your sentence that you're putting in the shift point of the entire story of creation now. This is ultimate newness! Feel it coming from the source of your being. Try to see if you have a sentence in there, written by the process of creation as uniquely you.

It's really awesome to imagine that your sentence—our sentence—is coming from the orchestra of evolution through us.

This, of course, speaks of the love for the impulse of creation itself, running through every one of us as our one sentence. It's very amazing to come up with a sentence.

As I'm going through this poem, if you want to, write a sentence that is written by the orchestra of evolution through you and as you. I haven't even thought of one myself yet. Your sentence, however, is not a random expression. **Your sentence is a Divine design, orchestrated by the inner and outer reality of the self-organizing Universe—conducting the symphony, weaving your unique word in the cosmic scroll.**

I think I have to read that again. Your sentence, that code that's coming through us through the entire process of creation, is a Divine design (not a random sentence) orchestrated by the inner and outer Reality of the self-organizing Universe. The self-organizing Universe is a new word for God, and we're using it because it seems to be able to cross all disciplines and doesn't necessarily relate to any specific discipline except the universal process itself.

Your sentence is orchestrated by the self-organizing Universe, conducting the symphony, Unique Self Symphony, weaving your unique word into the cosmic scroll.

I'm going to speak now about feeling the sentence inside ourselves as coming from the source of evolution, being spoken through us as an expression of our actual voice in the story of creation as us. If everybody's voice is literally an expression in the story of creation, feel into it for this moment.

Let's see what I feel in my voice. I really got very happy, Marc, when you said that this is the new lineage, and that everybody's voice is creating, for the first time on Earth, an evolutionary lineage. That the church of Evolutionary Love is a source of the new lineage of creation, meaning that everybody's unique voice is going to be amplified ever and ever more in Reality.

If you think of Moses who goes up to see God, we are like Moses going up, face to face, for the very first time, I believe. God didn't like to be seen face to face—never. It was always like, you could only see His back. **We are seeing God face to face because we have been given, by God—by a self-organizing Universe—the requirement to express God directly, face to face with each other**. We are being called to be the *voice that we are*, uniquely as us—but with no holds barred. I feel it personally when I have an opportunity to speak.

What I'm noticing is that if I can speak, and if you can speak with the voice of God as you, you will be activating others to do the same. Because in your presence, they will want to be the voice of God within them.

This chorus orchestrated by evolution that we're doing in the Evolutionary Church is an orchestration of the voices of God. It's now spoken by the voices of humanity saying *yes* to the impulse of creation within themselves, in the radically new church of Evolutionary Love that never existed before. I'm just acknowledging the radical newness of what we're doing.

I AM A UNIQUE CONFIGURATION OF INTIMACY THAT IS NEEDED BY ALL-THAT-IS

Can you feel that, everyone? *I am a unique configuration of intimacy that is needed by* All-That-Is! So, friends, I want to know what love is. You know what love is? Love is the knowing that I have a sentence. Now, there are parts of my sentence that are original; I have to find my original, unique sentence. **But the only way you can find your original, unique sentence is to first find the sentence that we all share.** Because what we all share in common is our uniqueness. Our uniqueness, as you know, is not our separateness. Our uniqueness is the realization that we are unique configurations of intimacy. It's more than no separation; we figured out no separation.

No separation takes me into oneness, but we have to go from oneness to unique expression of oneness.

Try and find this together. Let's actually see if we can join in this sentence, because when we join, that's where power is. *I'm a unique configuration of intimacy that's needed by All-That-Is.* That means I have a unique gift. If you can actually look in the mirror and know that's true…

121

- When I'm doing medicine, if I'm treating *unique configurations of intimacy that are needed by All-That-Is*, that changes all medicine.
- When I'm doing education, if I'm educating *unique configurations of intimacy that are needed by All-That-Is*.
- When I'm loving my friend, I'm loving a *unique configuration of intimacy that's needed by All-That-Is*.

That's true biologically. I'm biologically a unique configuration of amino acids and proteins. But in my interior, I'm a unique quality of intimacy that's needed by All-That-Is.

The promise will be kept! This is not just for us. This is for every one of us here—that this lights on fire in the world and becomes a flame. It's a flame, it's a cascading wave of Evolutionary Love that becomes a self-organizing Universe, that ignites Unique Self Symphonies and synergies. Not a top-down but a bottom-up self-organizing Universe, with each of us committing our Outrageous Acts of Love. That is the best hope for humanity at this moment in time.

CHAPTER TEN

BECOMING A WHOLE BEING: A UNIQUE COMBINATION OF LINES AND CIRCLES

Episode 150 — August 24, 2019

BEYOND HE AND SHE: THE TRANSGENDER QUESTION OF WHO AM I BENEATH MY GENDER?

Evolutionary Love Code:

> To awaken the new human and a new humanity, we require a gender liberation movement.

> We need to articulate and incarnate a new vision of evolutionary man and evolutionary woman.

> Evolutionary man and evolutionary woman understand the depth of the questions posed by the transgender movement, and they also understand the shallowness of the answers provided. Evolutionary man and woman are first Unique Self and Evolutionary Unique Self.

> From that deep ground of identity, evolutionary man and woman transition not to transgender, but to unique gender. Unique gender is a primary identifying characteristic of evolutionary man and woman.

Unique gender is not merely a balance between what were once called the masculine and the feminine traits. Rather, unique gender understands that the traits once identified as masculine and feminine are actually qualities of the Cosmos—what we refer to as Lines and Circles.

One's unique gender is an expression of one's Unique Self. **Unique gender is an emergent synergy from the unique integration of line and circle qualities in the human person.**

I want to just say a couple of words, then I want to invite Barbara to speak into this in this moment. But let's just try and find this—this is unbelievably important. What's the intuition?

I wrote about this in a couple of pages in a book that Kristina Kincaid and I put out called, *A Return to Eros*. It's a wonderful book about the radical experience of being fully alive. There's about four or five pages there on unique gender. Particularly as the leader of this project, Kristina is co-creating with me, the entire vision of the *Phenomenology of Eros*. Then there's a particular volume that Claire Molinard is stepping into, in a very deep way, called *Beyond He & She*. We're all working on that together.

What's *Beyond He & She*? This is so radically important, and we're going to hear from Barbara. Barbara this week is going to tell us a little bit about her own story in this. *I'm either he or she—is that true?*

The transgender movement says something very beautiful and very correct that's been said in different ways through history, but it's being said in a very potent way—now perhaps the most potent way:

- I'm not just a boy, and I'm not just a girl.
- I'm not exhausted by my boyness, and I'm not exhausted by my girlness.
- The fullness of who I am—I'm more whole than that.
- There is an identity to me that's underneath that identity.

I'm going to be very precise in the *dharma*. This is something new, so I want to ask everyone: *Don't let it drop into old categories you have.*

This is not balancing the masculine and feminine, this is something completely different.

Stay with it. In other words, my deep understanding of self is that *I'm not exhausted by the identities I've been given.* Let's say that I am a Frenchman; that's my identity. Let's say I'm Jewish; that's my identity. Let's say I'm Catholic; that's my identity. Let's say I'm Bulgarian; that's my identity. I'm Italian, or I'm Sicilian, or I'm from Montevideo; that's my identity.

Well, no! Because we're now realizing that doesn't exhaust my identity.

In the last 100 years, when people had an identity crisis, they broke out of their nationality. They broke out of their religion: *I'm more than just Jewish, I'm more than just Christian, I'm more than just Muslim.* That's the beginning of a worldcentric consciousness. Or *I'm more than French, I'm more than Sicilian, I'm more than Chinese, I'm more than Tibetan.*

We stepped beyond a kind of xenophobic nationalist patriotism as the sum total of our identity. That's important. Of course, we still need relationship to our country and to our tribe, which is beautiful. But we stepped beyond that. When we had an identity crisis, we broke out of that narrow identity.

Now, what identity remains for us? What do we have left?

We realized that *I'm not just Jewish, I'm not just Christian. I'm not just a particular nationality,* and *I'm not just a particular job—I'm not just a doctor or a lawyer.* So, what am I? What identity do I really still have? Oh—boy and girl! Someone's born: *it's a boy,* or *it's a girl.*

That's almost the only identity that remains: *I'm boy* and *I'm girl.*

But then we went deeper and we realized—and this is one of the great gifts of postmodernity—*I'm not just a boy and girl.*

Today, when we have an identity crisis, what do we do? We say, *well, I'm not a boy and girl.*

Imagine you're a 15-year-old and you're having an identity crisis. If you were a 15-year-old 40 years ago, and you were a Jewish kid growing up in the Bronx, and you had an identity crisis, you'd say: *I'm not just Jewish, I'm American.*

You break out of your old identity.

If you were an American kid 40 years ago, somewhere in the 60s, you'd say: *I'm not just American, I'm cosmopolitan.*

But when the only identity left is boy and girl, and we have an identity crisis, what happens? I want to break out of the only identity I have left, and what identity is that? *It's boy and girl*: that's all I have left. What's happening now around the world is: 15-year-old boys and girls are saying, oh my god, *I'm having an identity crisis*, but the only identity they have left is gender, so they go to break gender. They Google and see all sorts of posts in the transgender movement, which are really important and asking all the right questions.

They're challenging the limitation of *my identity as only a boy and only girl.* **What the transgender movement does is, it asks the right questions, and it senses there's a deeper identity beneath girl and boy.**

But that deeper identity doesn't mean that if I'm a girl, I should necessarily therefore change to a boy. *I'm going to throw away my girl identity, let me change to a boy*, or, *I'll throw away my boy identity, let me change to a girl.* I mean, occasionally, you might say that evolution made a mistake, and on a rare occasion, that might be a good thing to do.

I want to honor that. But that's not a pre-given move for 15-year-olds. It's not about changing to a different identity. *I'm a boy, now I'm going to be a girl.* Because you're going to wind up with all the problems of girl.

LINES AND CIRCLES ARE QUALITIES OF COSMOS THAT EXIST IN ALL OF US

Actually, it's deeper than that. I'm actually a unique gender.

I'm a unique emergent, which is the unique combination of what we call my line and circle quality.

My line is the masculine, my circle is the feminine; we call them line and circle because we don't want to fall into man and woman. These are qualities of Cosmos that exist in all of us.

The directional quality is one quality; the holding quality or the nurturing quality is a second quality. The directional quality is a line quality; the holding quality is a circle quality.

But those aren't man and woman qualities; we don't even want to call them masculine and feminine. They're qualities of Cosmos. Think London and New York: line is what used to be called masculine. Think Bali and Hawaii: circle, or feminine.

Now those qualities live in you and me together; they live in us, as us, and through us. **Line and circle qualities live in us uniquely, and there's a unique combination of those qualities**. That's called wholeness. So, who I am underneath boy and girl is not just my unique combination of boy and girl, it's my Unique Self. It's my Evolutionary Unique Self.

Who I am is:

+ I'm whole.
+ I'm *Homo amor*.
+ I'm a unique configuration.
+ I'm a person who incarnates divine purpose uniquely; and

that whole purpose, Evolutionary Unique Self *Homo amor universalis,* is beyond masculine and feminine, beyond he and she.

I have to bring together, not to balance my masculine and feminine, but to integrate my line and circle into something new that never was, is, or will be ever before. That's unique gender. We're talking about unique gender—*Homo amor.*

Let's bring Barbara in, to talk about her experience of her line and circle story—her story of line and circle, and this new moment of wholeness beyond.

THE EVOLUTION OF GENDER IS THE EVOLUTION INTO WHOLENESS

I remember the first stand about gender was to say to my father: *I'm sorry, I will not do what you say.* It was an awesome thing because there was nothing he could do about it. He wasn't going to kill me, he wasn't going to hit me, and I got the deal because he was such a dominant masculine. That was the touch of dealing with a very autocratic masculine, to stand up to it. That was the beginning of the feminine of, I would say, the evolutionary man or the creator man inside me.

Then, when we dropped the atomic bomb, I was surrounded by men who thought it was really great. The generals of the Second World War—the masculine—they won. That's when I realized, *Wait a minute, if we win more like that, we're all dead.*

I had a real interesting history of becoming a co-creator, which is, I had to say, *well, what is the meaning of this power to destroy and create like gods*? If you want to talk about creator, we are creators. Once we got that bomb, and now all the rest of it, the whole high-tech world is moving towards godlike power fast, and I could foresee it.

Then the great question was, *what is the meaning of this masculinity that's good?* This is a very great question, because a lot of people will totally criticize the masculine for this power and for the misuse of power, and not try to see what's great about it.

I intuitively began to have a Christ experience in the midst of this. In the Christ experience, basically the message was:

- Be me, I'm here for all of you. Barbara, if you can love God above all else, your neighbor as yourself, yourself as me a natural Christ.
- Now, that's neither masculine or feminine. Combined with science and technology, you will all be changed.
- I would like demonstrations now, Barbara. Could you demonstrate what it's like to inherit the power of the Christ? To say that's who I am, and that's who you are.

That was the entire message of Christ: *If you've seen me, you've seen the Father; if you've seen the Father, you've seen the mother.* So, I became what I would call a *natural Christ impulse.*

It was in there, combined at that time with my friendship with Jonas Salk, who took me down to these biology labs, where they were saying: *stamp out physical death.* At the same time, I was reading the Bible, where Jesus was doing all these miracles, including the resurrection from the dead. So I would ask, *How can we do the resurrection from the dead?* It turns out, we're doing it. It turns out, if you really go to the leading edge of science, in the biological realm, they know how to resurrect little strands of DNA, and they're on their way to it.

In fact, I had a friend who invented molecular nanotechnology, and he called me out right on the phone without any introduction.

He said, "Barbara, I think we can do resurrection."

I said, "Well, it's about time."

He said, "What do you mean it's about time?"

I said, "Well, the reason it's about time is because that's what Jesus said: You will do the work that I do, and greater works. So, you folks, you've taken the time to do it, thank you."

Eric Drexler[4] was his name, he invented molecular nanotechnology.

Here's the next thing that happened. I am actually a total example of the incarnation of both of those—I wonder if the other women have this. Along with having incarnated the impulse of creation and being a *natural Christ* and believing that we're going to have the powers that Christ had, I wanted to please men.

I talked this over with my sister Patricia Ellsberg,[5] who's married to Daniel Ellsberg, and who's a pretty strong man too. I was at that time 25 years with Sydney. I noticed that when I talked to Sydney, I had a kind of baby voice. *Hi, Sydney, how are you?*

So, here, this woman who was incarnating the Christ and going to resurrect from the dead was trying to please men. This woman who feels very masculine, but somehow wants to please men, in a kind of babyish way—not to please a man like I would try to please you, Marc. Of course I would try to please you, because I love you. But it's very different from that babyish voice. I talked it over with my sister, Patricia, who is also a very strong woman. Every time she talks to Daniel Ellsberg, she has a babyish voice.

That made me really realize that way down deep inside the desire of the feminine—and I am very feminine in many ways—is to please the man. Then I saw, if we weren't able to please the man in the early stages

---

4   Eric Drexler is an American engineer, author, and futurist best known for his pioneering work in the field of molecular nanotechnology—the concept of building machines at the atomic or molecular scale.

5   Patricia Ellsberg is an American activist, writer, and former radio journalist best known for her involvement in peace activism and for being the wife of Daniel Ellsberg, the former U.S. military analyst who famously leaked the Pentagon Papers in 1971.

of evolution, they probably would've left us and the babies would've died. Because the real difference between men and women is, women have babies; that's really the difference. It's not just a gender difference. It's a total physicality and psycho-spiritual difference.

When a woman is pregnant, she absolutely has to keep the man. Because most men don't really like it when the woman is all that pregnant; they've lost their mate to some degree. During the pregnancy, the woman has learned to keep the man. If she didn't, they left her and the babies died.

So, I think that there is something deep in the feminine that has to do with pregnancy, and giving birth, and needing the man not only to impregnate her but to care for her during the birth and right after the birth, and care for that baby because she can't do it.

We are all the descendants of women who could keep men by being totally pleasing. Now the question is, what to do now? We're not having babies right now. We're not trying to keep men we love by pleasing them because we're pregnant.

I want to just take it to the next step here. The way I feel that I have become whole, if I may say that, is by saying a profound *yes* to purpose. The purpose inside any of us is neither masculine nor feminine. **A genuine life purpose is beyond masculine and feminine.**

I'm not talking about the type of purpose of keeping the man and pleasing him.

I'm very strong, and I know what the difference is. But the purpose is express the inner impulse of evolution, to shift the world from devolution to evolution. That is not masculine or feminine—that's whole.

I have begun to say that: *What really becomes the whole being, I believe, is an incarnation of the impulse of the Divine as you, as your purpose. Then you say yes to that impulse, and the impulse is not masculine or feminine.*

If you think of going through the core of the spiral, that's not man or woman—that's not masculine or feminine. God really is neither masculine or feminine. **Spirit, God, or Source is not masculine or feminine.**

The woman can incarnate the impulse and say *100% yes*, no matter how it affects the men around her. They might not like it, and a lot of men don't really like it if a woman is that passionate about her purpose. But if she is, and she still has that yearning for the masculine love, it is really good. I mean, I'm glad I feel that way.

We're becoming a new species: *Homo amor universalis*. What I've been able to understand about being a member of *Homo amor universalis* is the word *whole*. **I feel like my masculine and my feminine, my inner and my outer, my life purpose and other people's life purposes, have become whole**. I feel the awesome Reality that the species that we're calling *Homo amor universalis* has been able to do what humanity has not been able to do at all. Because *Homo sapiens sapiens* does not bring together science and heart and love and beauty. *Homo amor universalis* has become whole as an entire species. The awesome power of the wholeness of *Homo amor universalis* is species-wide.

We can in this church, both the women and the men, experience ourselves as *Homo amor universalis,* which is whole. It's even more than integrated, it is wholeness. When I say this and speak this, I actually feel that I am a new being, that the wholeness is new.

How does Reality create newness? It creates new wholes, like single-cell to multi-cell to animal to human.

A whole being—*Homo amor universalis*—is more than a good *Homo sapiens sapiens.*

As a whole woman integrating masculine and feminine, and integrating the divine expression of creativity or God as purpose, I know that God's purpose incarnates as each one of us.

Oh my god, what is this type? I think we have to say *Yes* to the evolution of gender, but the evolution of gender ultimately is the evolution of the person into wholeness.

The notion of unique gender beyond boy and girl is that there is a wholeness that lives underneath gender.

Underneath gender, we're whole—we're *Homo amor*.

We express and find that wholeness and unique gift by finding the precise integration of our line and circle qualities, which come together to create the *Hieros Gamos*—to create the wholeness that is ever, and always, and already there.

Underneath gender is not boy becomes girl or girl becomes boy. It's actually a line-circle. It's beyond he and she.

Beyond he and she is *Homo amor*.

APPENDIX: SONGS

THE BATTLE HYMN OF THE REPUBLIC—JULIA WARD HOWE[1]

Mine eyes have seen the glory of the coming of the Lord.

He has trampled down the vintage
  where the grapes of wrath are stored.

He has loosed the fateful lightning
  of his terrible swift sword.

His truth is marching on.

HOW COULD ANYONE—LIBBY RODERICK[2]

How could anyone ever tell you
  you were anything less than beautiful?

How could anyone ever tell you
  you were less than whole?

How could anyone fail to notice
  that your loving is a miracle—
  how deeply you're connected to my soul?

---

1 Julia Ward Howe, The Battle Hymn of the Republic, 1862.
2 Libby Roderick, "How Could Anyone," on *If You See a Dream* (Turtle Island Records, 1990), CD.

I WANT TO KNOW WHAT LOVE IS—FOREIGNER[3]

I've gotta take a little time,
a little time to think things over.
I better read between the lines,
in case I need it when I'm older.
(Whoa, ooh-ooh, ooh-ooh)

And this mountain, I must climb
feels like the world upon my shoulders,
and through the clouds, I see love shine,
it keeps me warm as life grows colder.

[Pre-Chorus]
In my life, there's been heartache and pain.
I don't know if I can face it again.
Can't stop now, I've travelled so far
to change this lonely life.

[Chorus]
I wanna know what love is.
I want you to show me.
I wanna feel what love is.
I know you can show me.
Oh, oh-oh, oh (ooh)

I'm gonna take a little time,
a little time to look around me.
I've got nowhere left to hide,
it looks like love has finally found me.

[Pre-Chorus]

[Chorus]

[Outro]

(And I wanna feel) I wanna feel what love is

3   Foreigner, "I Want To Know What Love Is," recorded November 1984, on *Agent Provocateur*, Atlantic Records, vinyl LP.

(And I know) I know you can show me.
Let's talk about love.
(I wanna know what love is) The love that you feel inside.
(I want you to show me) And I'm feelin' so much love.
(I wanna feel what love is) No, you just cannot hide.
(I know you can show me) Yeah.
I wanna know what love is (Let's talk about love).
I want you to show me, I wanna feel.
(I wanna feel what love is) And I know, and I know.
I know you can show me (Yeah).
(I wanna know what love is) (I wanna know)
(I want you to show me) I wanna know, I wanna know, wanna know.
(I wanna feel what love is) (I wanna feel)
(I know you can show me).

HALLELUJAH—LEONARD COHEN[4]

Now, I've heard there was a secret chord
that David played, and it pleased the Lord.
But you don't really care for music, do you?
It goes like this, the fourth, the fifth,
the minor fall, the major lift.
The baffled king composing Hallelujah.

[Chorus]

Hallelujah, Hallelujah,
Hallelujah, Hallelujah.

Your faith was strong, but you needed proof.
You saw her bathing on the roof.
Her beauty and the moonlight overthrew you.
She tied you to a kitchen chair,
she broke your throne, and she cut your hair,
and from your lips she drew the Hallelujah.

---

4 Leonard Cohen, "Hallelujah", Various Positions, Columbia Records, 1984, LP.

[Chorus]

You say I took the name in vain,
I don't even know the name,
but if I did, well, really, what's it to you?
There's a blaze of light in every word,
it doesn't matter which you heard,
the holy or the broken Hallelujah.

[Chorus]

I did my best, it wasn't much.
I couldn't feel, so I tried to touch.
I've told the truth, I didn't come to fool you.
And even though it all went wrong,
I'll stand before the Lord of Song
With nothing on my tongue but Hallelujah.

OM NAMAH SHIVAAYA

Om Namah Shivaaya
Shivaaya namaha,
Shivaaya namah om
Shivaaya namaha, namaha Shivaaya
Shambhu Shankara namah Shivaaya,
Girijaa Shankara namah Shivaaya
Arunaachala Shiva namah Shivaaya

I bow to the soul of all. I bow to my Self. I don't know who I am, so I bow to you, Shiva, my own true Self. I bow to my teachers who loved me with love. Who took care of me when I couldn't take care of myself. I owe everything to them. How can I repay them? They have everything in the world. Only my love is mine to give, but in giving I find that it is their love flowing through me back to the world...I have nothing. I have everything. I want nothing. Only let it flow to you, my love... sing!

INDEX

sacred 3, 34, 86
sangha 40
second-person 8, 18, 30, 31, 48, 59, 60, 73, 85, 86, 87
security 70
self-organizing 34, 40, 48, 58, 89, 90, 116, 119, 120, 122
separate self 22, 66, 85
separation 23, 64, 77, 121
service 35, 74, 76, 88, 89, 90, 91
sexual 59
sexuality 56
shadow 35, 74, 108
Shakti 75
shame 36
shards 13, 46, 117
shefa 75
Solomon 4, 7, 28, 47, 113
soul 23, 50, 98, 116
soul mate 50, 98, 116
Source 39, 73, 108, 131
source code 18, 28, 31, 33, 39, 40, 41, 47, 79, 109, 110, 112, 115, 117
Spirit 13, 60, 84, 87, 131
story 2, 3, 4, 5, 8, 9, 11, 13, 15, 16, 23, 27, 33, 36, 38, 41, 45, 47, 55, 56, 57, 58, 65, 70, 71, 82, 83, 88, 93, 98, 101, 104, 108, 109, 112, 119, 120, 124, 128
St. Paul 40
structure of Reality 88, 94
structures 28, 71, 110
Sufism 86, 87
synagogue 44, 72, 84, 114
synergy 92, 110, 124

T

Talmud 75
tenderness 6, 49, 59, 76, 100
the One 15, 21, 40, 41, 44, 60, 72, 84, 86, 97, 108, 114
the Universe 29, 58, 61, 83, 115, 116
The Universe

A Love Story 16, 92
The whole 4, 5, 10, 20, 21, 22, 24, 25, 26, 33, 38, 46, 74, 78, 79, 83, 86, 89, 91, 92, 94, 95, 97, 98, 100, 101, 116, 128, 131, 132, 133
third-person 7, 30, 48, 60, 73, 84, 86, 114
Thou Art That 60
Three Faces of God 19
Tillich, Paul 46, 83
tov 87, 114
traditions 33, 60, 75, 83, 86, 114
tragic 74
transformation 27, 28, 32, 34, 35, 36, 38, 39, 44, 45, 53, 55, 71, 72, 98, 102
transgender 123, 124, 126
transmission 40, 86
tribe 88, 94, 125
trinity 60
True Self 34
truth 13, 23, 56, 60, 61, 83, 94, 102, 108

U

understanding 9, 15, 16, 18, 33, 85, 91, 97, 102, 104, 123, 125, 132
unguarded 25
unique gender 123, 124, 126, 128, 132
unique gift 5, 8, 35, 41, 51, 71, 74, 75, 121, 133
unique intimacy 53
uniqueness 5, 9, 51, 64, 78, 101, 121
Unique Self 4, 5, 16, 23, 24, 29, 34, 35, 40, 54, 66, 69, 71, 74, 75, 78, 90, 106, 111, 117, 118, 120, 122, 123, 124, 127
Unique Self Symphony 5, 12, 29, 40, 54, 69, 71, 74, 78, 90, 106, 116, 118, 119, 120, 122
unique voice 116, 117, 120

INDEX

ABOUT THE AUTHORS

Dr. Marc Gafni is a visionary world philosopher and futurist, one of the leading formulators of world spirituality and religion of our time, and a beloved teacher and public intellectual. He holds his doctorate in philosophy from Oxford University, as well as Orthodox rabbinic ordination. He co-founded the activist think tank, now called the Center for World Philosophy and Religion where he serves as the co-president with Dr. Zachary Stein. He also served with Barbara Marx Hubbard as co-president of the Foundation for Conscious Evolution, which he consented to lead at Barbara's request after her passing.

He is known for his "source code teachings"—including Unique Self theory and the Five Selves, the Amorous Cosmos, a Politics of Evolutionary Love, a Return to Eros, and Digital Intimacy—and has more than twenty books to his name, including the award-winning Your Unique Self, A Return to Eros, and three volumes of Radical Kabbalah.

He teaches on the cutting edge of philosophy in the West, helping to evolve a new "*dharma*" or meta-theory of Integral meaning that is helping to re-shape key pivoting points in global consciousness and culture, with the aim of participating in the articulation of what Dr. Gafni together with Dr. Stein and colleagues are calling CosmoErotic Humanism.

At the core of CosmoErotic Humanism is what Dr. Gafni and Dr. Stein are calling First Principles and First Values, Anthro-Ontology, and a Universal Grammar of Value. This is the ground of a new shared universe story and a new narrative of identity for the new human and the new humanity. This is what they are calling the emergence from Homo sapiens to *Homo amor*.

This shared story rooted in First Principles and First Values can then serve as the matrix for a global ethos for a global civilization.

Together with Dr. Stein and Ken Wilber, Gafni is writing a series of seminal books under the collective pseudonym of David J. Temple, which intend to evolve the source code of consciousness and culture in response to the meta-crisis. The first of those books is *First Principles and First Values: Forty-Two Propositions on CosmoErotic Humanism, the Meta-Crisis, and the World to Come.*

Barbara Marx Hubbard (born Barbara Marx; December 22, 1929–April 10, 2019) was an American futurist, author, and public speaker. She is credited with the Wheel of Co-Creation and together with Dr. Gafni, the Wheel of Co-Creation 2.0, as well as the concepts of the Synergy Engine and the "birthing" of humanity.

As co-founder and president of the Foundation for Conscious Evolution and the chair, for the last five years of her life, of the Center for World Philosophy and Religion, she posited that humanity was on the threshold of a quantum leap if newly emergent scientific, social, and spiritual capacities were integrated to address global crises.

She was the author of seven books on social and planetary evolution. In conjunction with the Shift Network, she co-produced the worldwide "Birth 2012" multimedia event. She was also the subject of a biography by author Neale Donald Walsch, *The Mother of Invention: The Legacy of Barbara Marx Hubbard.* Deepak Chopra called her "the voice for conscious evolution."

In 1984, she was symbolically nominated for the vice presidency of the United States. She also co-chaired a number of Soviet-American Citizen Summits, introducing a new concept called SYNCON, to foster synergistic convergence with opposing groups. In addition, she co-founded the World Future Society and the Association for Global New Thought.

Volume 15 — Evolutionary Church

LIST OF EPISODES

9 798888 340639